IN THE
PRESENCE
OF THE
POOR

IN THE
PRESENCE
OF THE
POOR

CHANGING THE FACE OF INDIA

KAY MARSHALL STROM

Authentic

COLORADO SPRINGS • MILTON KEYNES • HYDERABAD

Authentic Publishing
We welcome your questions and comments.

USA   1820 Jet Stream Drive, Colorado Springs, CO 80921
         www.authenticbooks.com
UK   9 Holdom Avenue, Bletchley, Milton Keynes, Bucks, MK1 1QR
         www.authenticmedia.co.uk
India   Logos Bhavan, Medchal Road, Jeedimetla Village, Secunderabad
         500 055, A.P.

In the Presence of the Poor
ISBN-13: 978-1-60657-012-8

11 10 09 / 6 5 4 3 2 1

All Scripture quotations, unless otherwise indicated, are taken from the *Holy Bible,
New International Version*®. *NIV*®. Copyright © 1973, 1978, 1984 by International
Bible Society. Used by permission of Zondervan. All rights reserved.

A catalog record for this book is available through the Library of Congress.

Cover design: James Hershberger
Interior design: projectluz.com
Editorial team: Bette Smyth, Dana Bromley, Mary Lou White

Printed in the United States of America

CONTENTS

FOREWORD

There is no shortage of books about *Western* missionary heroes. What the global Christian church lacks are books about *indigenous* missionary heroes. Thankfully, Kay Marshall Strom has taken a step to rectify that imbalance with this book about a missionary *from* India *to* India, a man whom I am privileged to call a friend.

Known to many simply as "Viji," Dr. B. E. Vijayam (which means "victory") fits the classic definition of pioneer—he is breaking new ground in missionary practice. I have often teased him about the alphabet soup he has created—TENT, JVI, PROGRESS, IWILL, and others. But each acronym represents an innovative and creative approach to reaching India with God's love.

Dr. Viji, born the son and grandson of prominent Christian bishops, gained his reputation as a nationally recognized scientist. This book will take you through that story, one that easily matches any you have read about how God calls people to serve him.

Today, Dr. Viji's creativity is focused at a retreat/study complex called Carmel, located about twelve miles (twenty kilometers) outside the city of Hyderabad, India. Here, Joshua Vision India (JVI) prepares teams of Master Trainers, each of whom researches a particular unreached people group and then develops a church-planting strategy for it. But JVI doesn't stop there. At Carmel Dr. Viji has gathered a small army of his scientist friends to explore simple, appropriate, and cutting-edge technologies. These technologies are taught to church-planting teams as a means of supporting themselves in the field as well as benefiting the people of India whom they serve.

As he showed me around the Carmel campus, I was astounded at what I saw: plants that have the potential to produce bio-diesel fuel; worms that transform cow dung into odorless, dry fertilizer; a special, protein-rich range grass that survives in arid places and fattens cows and goats at twice the normal rate; and workshop-based technologies such as candle-making, silk-screening, and guard-dog training. There is even a research center that maps India's people groups using the latest global positioning technology.

What is important, however, is not the technological creativity, but the motivation behind the creativity: to bring the good news of God's kingdom to the 4,600 people groups of India. It takes a big vision to accomplish big things, and it takes a big-hearted person to lead the way. Fortunately for India, Dr. Viji has both.

May you be blessed by this account of a true indigenous missionary hero and, at the same time, personally challenged by how much God can accomplish through a life that is clearly focused on honoring Him.

—Jon Lewis
President/CEO of Partners International

PROLOGUE TO
NORTH
AMERICANS

I flew into Calcutta in October—the Hindu month of Ashwin, the time of *Diwali,* the festival of lights. The Season of the Gods is what they call it in India. Summer's smothering heat finally loosens its relentless grip, and with the blessed breeze come days of feasting and dancing and music. I pressed my head against the small glass pane and stared out, but all I could see through the airplane window was darkness. Then the plane made a dip and a sharp turn, and suddenly an endless expanse of light spread out before me in spectacular array.

"Do not be fooled by the season," the turbaned man seated beside me stated. "India is a country without hope." I turned and stared at him in surprise.

"I only come back once a year, just to see my parents," he continued. "Only because it is expected of me. Could I choose,

5

I would never return. What has the mother-goddess done for this country? What have all the millions of Hindu gods and goddesses together done for us?"

For five days I had been in India, just long enough to get a taste of Indian reality. Devastating poverty. Beggars flooding the sidewalks or pressing their faces against car windows to plead for coins. Chaotic traffic with horns blaring nonstop at motorbikes, oxcarts, pedestrians, bicycles, and three-wheeled auto-rickshaws that clog the narrow road—but always yield the right-of-way to cows. Ever-present ragged children rummaging through garbage piles in search of food. Festival firecrackers and beating drums surrounding shrines erected on every corner. Garlands of marigolds and offerings of fresh fruit, incense, and burning candles decorating the shrines, each with an idol staring out. And everywhere, people, people, people, in all places and at all hours.

Chances are, you have never been to India. You may well have no plans to go. Even so, whether you realize it or not, you almost certainly encounter India regularly. Have you ever had an appliance malfunction and called for technical assistance? Most likely, that voice on the other end of the phone line—the one with the unfamiliar accent—was an Indian speaking to you from Mumbai or Bangalore. If your call was about your computer, you probably talked to someone in India. Should you have the misfortune to be struck with a sudden illness and have to be rushed to the emergency room, you may be greeted by a dark-skinned doctor who speaks to you with that same accent. If you are a business person or a student, or if you work in a technological field, enjoy movies or the theater, or buy clothes for a good price, you likely have experienced India reaching out and touching your life. In the twenty-first century, East has already met West.

I first visited India in 2002. I had prepared myself by reading about the slums, the poverty, and Mother Teresa and her work in Calcutta. I also read about the outsourcing of North American jobs and about what it means to be a Christian in a country hostile to the gospel. But I wasn't in India long before I was struck by the woeful simplicity of all my preparation. What I found was a vast country of blinding contrasts and bewildering contradictions. And with each subsequent visit, I find more and more examples of these.

India is undergoing a dramatic transformation, but that transformation has not reached the majority of Indians. The entire information technology industry employs only about 800,000 people, a tiny percent of the country's 1.1 billion people. In 2008 India boasted twenty-three billionaires, despite the fact that over 80 percent of the country's population survives on less than the equivalent of $2 (U.S.) a day. Million-dollar apartments overlook an almost endless expanse of slums. In fact, Mumbai (Bombay) has the dubious distinction of being home to the largest slum in the world. And in 2008, even as the Indian economy entered its fourth year of rapid expansion, making it one of the world's fastest growing economies, still two out of every three people in India lacked clean drinking water.

Three thousand years after the emergence of the caste system, stark class divisions define almost every area of Indian society—from the quality of education available to marriage prospects, job potential, one's personal value, and even the right to exist. While I was in the country, a distinguished bishop of the Church of South India—a well-educated, fine-spoken man with a Ph.D., who risks his life to argue before Parliament on behalf of the rights of the Dalits—walked down the street past a woman laborer. She spends her days sitting on the side of the road, through the sweltering heat of the hot season and the pouring rains of the monsoons, hammering piles of rocks into handmade gravel. As the bishop passed, the woman glanced up with disdain and spit at him, because he is of a lower caste than she.

Contrasts? Yes. Contradictions? Shocking and numerous. But a country without hope? Not at all.

—Kay Marshall Strom

CHAPTER 1
HOW IT
ALL BEGAN

Tiny Vijayam gazed over the side of his father's rough-hewn bullock cart as it bounced across the untamed Indian countryside. Traveling with his family from one oppressed village to the next was the only life the little boy knew. Day after day, he watched as they rumbled past ragged men and women trudging along sun-scorched trails, balancing huge loads on their heads. Field after field, he passed men and women laboring under harsh taskmasters, through searing heat or monsoon rains. And always there were beggars, skinny children, and mothers cradling starving babies, all crying out for food.

"Why does God make so many poor people?" Vijayam asked. "Why, Papa, why?" No answer his father offered could satisfy the little boy.

It was into a rare Indian family that Vijayam Edmund Bunyan was born on November 20, 1933—rare in that they were devout Christians. Vijayam's grandfather had converted from Hinduism years before. Back then, during a time of severe famine, a British army officer by the name of Waters had watched helplessly as desperate Indians fled their homes in search of food. Determined to do something, he provided food, water, and shelter for as many as he possibly could. And being a devout Christian, he also told them of God's love for them. When Officer Waters was transferred from the area, he invited about one hundred Indians to go with him. One of those was an orphan boy who took the names Gideon (after the biblical character) and Bunyan (after John Bunyan, author of *Pilgrim's Progress*). Through teachings from the Bible, Gideon Bunyan had come to understand that salvation comes only through Jesus Christ and that idols have no place in Christianity. This convert was Vijayam's grandfather.

Like other early Indian Christians, Gideon Bunyan learned to speak, read, and write in English, which made him extremely well educated for his day. In those days, no roads connected one isolated village of thatched-roof huts with another. So Gideon Bunyan, one of the first Christian missionaries in that part of India, trudged on foot over rugged hills and through tiger and cobra-infested jungles as he carried the message of God's love from village to village.

Vijayam's father, Bunyan Joseph, was the twelfth of Gideon Bunyan's sixteen children. Although Joseph grew up knowing about Jesus Christ, one question continually plagued him: *If I die tomorrow, what will happen to me—will I actually reach heaven?*

In those days, few Indians were Christians. Perhaps the most well known was an Indian Christian holy man, Sundar Singh. Born in 1889 into great wealth and privilege in the Punjab, Sundar Singh had every comfort a man could desire. He had everything except happiness and peace, and the quest for these consumed him. Desperately, he sought to know God. Not to know *about* God, but to truly *know* him. Finally, at the age of sixteen, disappointed and discouraged, Sundar gave up his search. He preferred to die rather than live one more day without God. Every afternoon at exactly four o'clock, the train passed in front of Sundar Singh's house. In despair he determined that he would lie down on the tracks and end his life. But just as he was about to carry out his plan, Jesus appeared to him in a vision. His search came to an end that day, and from that moment on, Sundar Singh followed Jesus passionately.

Sundar Singh's father, not at all pleased at the change in his son, ordered the young man to renounce Jesus Christ. When Sundar refused, his father drove him from his home and family, away from everything he knew and held dear. So Sundar adopted the life of a sadhu (Hindu ascetic), donning the traditional saffron robe and walking barefoot throughout northern India carrying the gospel of Jesus Christ. (Because he walked barefoot through the Himalayas with his message, he was popularly known as the Apostle of the Bleeding Feet.)

"Christianity is the fulfillment of Hinduism," Sadhu Sundar Singh told the people. "Hinduism has been digging channels. Christ is the water to flow through those channels . . . . There are many beautiful things in Hinduism; but the fullest light is from Jesus Christ."

As he traveled the countryside, the Christian sadhu told the story of a high caste Hindu man overcome by the beating summer sun. Exhausted almost to the point of unconsciousness, he slumped down in a seat at a railway station. An employee, seeing the man's plight, ran to a nearby well and filled the common cup with water; then he rushed it to the desperate man. But the Hindu raised his hand and weakly waved the cup away, wishing to die rather than touch his lips to a cup that might have been used by someone of a lower caste. Only then did a passerby notice that the Hindu had his own cup lying on the seat beside him. Quickly, the man rushed to the well and filled the cup with water; then he hurried it back to the gasping Hindu man who gratefully gulped it down.

"This is what I tell the missionaries who come to us from abroad," Sadhu Sundar Singh explained. "You have been offering the water of life to the people of India in a foreign cup. That is why we have been slow to receive it. If you offer it to us in an Indian cup we are more likely to accept it." When Hindus saw Sundar Singh in his saffron-colored robe, they immediately bowed their heads in respect. "But you are a Christian," the Christians objected. "Why do you wear the saffron robe of an Indian holy man?" The sadhu replied, "Because the gospel should be given to Indians in an Indian cup."

Gideon Bunyan knew this story well—and so did his son Joseph. Like the sadhu's other exploits and teachings, it was told again and again. Then word spread that the great Sadhu Sundar

Singh would be coming to Andhra Pradesh, in fact, to the very area where Joseph and his family lived. Joseph could hardly wait. He was most eager to meet the great teacher and to ask of him the question that burned in his heart.

Many people asked questions of the sadhu that day. But when Joseph had his chance, he asked, "Sadhu, if people ask me, 'Are you saved,' what should I say?" Sundar Singh replied, "I say, 'I'm saved, but not safe.'"

Joseph went home contemplating those words, *Saved, but not safe*. As he thought on them, Jesus appeared to him in a vision and showed his nail-scarred hands. Then Joseph exclaimed, "Yes! I *am* saved!" The question that had haunted him for so long was at last settled—forever.

Following the sadhu's lead, Bunyan Joseph determined that he, too, would be a man dedicated to God. So he also dressed in a saffron robe, and he went to the forest where he spent months alone reading the Bible, meditating, and praying. When he returned, he preached with great power—presenting the gospel to the people of India in an Indian cup.

Material things never mattered to Bunyan Joseph. Food to eat and a shirt on his back were enough for him. His passion was simply to tell others about his Savior. He married Lucy Prakashmani, a young woman who shared his passion. She was the third daughter of the first pastor in the large Kurnool district of the same Indian state, and she, too, was educated, an especially rare thing for a woman in those days.

After their wedding, Joseph attended theological school. He then served as a village pastor and the principal of a small theological school on the eastern edge of the Nallamala hills, in the state of Andhra Pradesh. Bunyan Joseph had a heart full of mercy and was drawn to the poorest people around him. In a society where castes stayed strictly in their places and where life and death were never far apart, he worked among the most desperate of the people.

In those days smallpox was the scourge of India. One day as Joseph returned home from visiting a man sick with smallpox, his tiny son toddled out to meet him. Joseph scooped up the child and, hugging him close, carried him back to the house. In the middle of the night the boy awoke with a raging fever. By morning he bore the unmistakable signs of the dreaded pox. Joseph never contracted the disease, but he had unwittingly carried it home to his son. Within days his firstborn was dead. Despite his grief Joseph continued his ministry of compassion, because the people had no one else.

Of the eight children Joseph and Lucy had, only five survived: sons Hosea, Abhishekam, Azariah, and Vijayam and daughter Margret Sowbhagyam. Vijayam, the youngest, was often told, "You are a gift from God, our son. You are a miracle. For you never should have survived your first day of life."

It was true. Lucy, in labor in a small jungle hospital that November day in 1933, knew something wasn't right. It was her eighth child, and this birth was not like the others. "Breech," the doctor told Joseph. "The baby is backwards. I will have to kill it in order to save your wife."

"No!" Joseph insisted. "I will ask God to perform a miracle. I am certain that both my wife and my son will live." The doctor, who did not share the evangelist's faith, made preparations to cut the baby apart. But suddenly, to the doctor's amazement, the baby did a somersault and was born naturally. When the doctor told Joseph what had happened, Joseph shouted, "Vijayam!" In the Telugu language, *vijayam* means "victory." That, he said, would be the baby's name. The doctor added the middle name, Edmund.

When Vijayam was young, his father was assigned to a remote area of southern India to plant churches. Joseph's salary was to be twenty-five rupees a month, a good amount in those days. But like every other pastor, he was told, "It is up to you to collect your pay from your parishioners." Joseph looked around at the poverty-stricken people who made up his new flock. Precious little stood between them and starvation. What did they have to spare? How could he possibly ask them to give what they did not have? "No," he said to those over him. "You don't have to pay me anything."

Joseph built a wooden cart that could be pulled by two bullocks. Then he packed up his family and headed to the isolated villages. They were away for weeks at a time. And so it was that from his earliest days Vijayam bore witness to the great suffering of India's poor and oppressed. Villagers who existed on one meal a day of rice shared the little they had with the evangelist and his family. With clean water scarce in the primitive villages and with no medical facilities available, Vijayam suffered in turn from pneumonia, malaria, and typhoid fever—all diseases usually fatal in those pre-penicillin days. His only medicines were the fervent prayers of his family and their tender nursing and care. It was all they had to give him.

Bunyan Joseph's approach was the same in each village. He began by helping the men build a mud house for worship. Then he unfolded the life of Jesus before the people through the songs and plays he wrote. After that, he preached the gospel. Then always, before he left a village, he taught the men a trade so they could earn money to feed their families—sustainability, before it was a popular Western concept.

For years Joseph carried on his innovative approach to the ministry, assisted by his wife and growing family. Each summer he organized village fairs, and people flocked in from some fifty surrounding villages. With piles of mangoes and huge pots of rice, no one went hungry. Between the preaching sessions, everyone participated in drama competitions, and afterward they sang through the night. Only when the fingers of dawn finally reached across the sky did they give in and stretch out under the trees for a few hours of sleep.

No one who came to Bunyan Joseph's door ever went away hungry. For however great the needs of his own family, he was well aware that they paled in comparison to the grinding desperation of the starving poor all around. Vijayam and his brothers and sister grew up weaving baskets and raising poultry to help support the family.

Still, there were times when even this wasn't enough. One day there was no food left in the house, so Vijayam's mother, Lucy, did the only thing she knew to do—she joined the field laborers heading to the fields to work. As she approached, the landlord stared at her. She didn't look at all like a common laborer.

"Whose daughter are you?" the landlord asked her. When Lucy told him, the landlord exclaimed, "What? My family bought this land from your father! I can't make you work. You go sit down in the shade." She tried to argue, but the landowner wouldn't listen. "I insist!" he said.

At noon the landlord brought food to her. As soon as he was out of sight, she carefully tucked it away in her bag to share with her family for dinner. When Lucy was ready to leave, the landlord pressed two rupees into her hand—a man's wages for a full day's work. "This is too great a miracle!" Lucy sighed.

Then, on the way home from the field, she found a ten-rupee note lying on the path. "Another gift from God!" Lucy exclaimed, and she hurried home to tell her husband about the day's blessings and give him the twelve rupees.

Now Bunyan Joseph was a singularly uncompromising man. He made great sacrifices for the high principles by which he lived, and he expected his family to do the same. After he heard his wife's story, Joseph told her, "This is not our money. We must find the owner and give it back." Lucy gasped in disbelief. "But how can we possibly find the owner?"

"If we can't find him," Joseph said, "we will put the money in the offering. We must not keep what is not ours." Joseph's word was the last word; so despite the family's need, what he said was done.

Three days later an unexpected money order arrived from England. It was a royalty payment on the English translation of a play Joseph had written years before. The amount was twelve rupees.

Great Britain brought organized Christianity to India in the nineteenth century. As time passed, however, Indian Christians spent more time quibbling over differences between denominations than on preaching the gospel or aiding the poor. "How can we present Christ if we are so busy arguing and quarreling among ourselves?" Bunyan Joseph protested. "Anglican, Presbyterian, Congregational, Methodist—we don't need all these denominations. What we need is one church for India!"

This idea did not please the British. They saw the call for an Indian church as a nationalistic stand. In their opinion, Indian Christians should keep out of anything that even remotely smacked of politics. But it was too late. The movement was already on.

The year was 1946, and the talk throughout India was of Mahatma Gandhi and the push toward independence from Britain. In May of that year, as thirteen-year-old Vijayam and his family were preparing for bed, a telegram arrived at their bungalow. As soon as Bunyan Joseph and his wife read it, they fell to their knees in prayer. "Thank you, Father, for these great blessings," Joseph prayed aloud before his perplexed children. "Make me worthy of this call." The telegram read: *You have been selected the first bishop of the newly formed Church of South India.*

In August 1947 India attained independence from British rule. Two months later in the Rayalseema Diocese (the southern part of Andhra Pradesh), Bunyan Joseph was consecrated the first bishop of the Church of South India.

One church, free of discord and distractions, was the dream. But politics are everywhere, and the church is no exception. Divisions had already begun to develop. "Hindu country, Christian country, it is all the same," says Hosea Bunyan, Joseph's oldest son. "Where there is too much personal ambition, there is no room for the gospel."

As bishop, Bunyan Joseph held authority over every church institution, and he would stay in that position of authority until he relinquished it in writing. Increasingly, however, parties within the church pressured him to hand over control to the wrong people. He resisted the pressure and refused.

But the time came when the church that Bishop Bunyan Joseph had worked so hard to help establish became his enemy. So finally in submission he wrote, "It is not for me. It is not for me." Then he moved his family out of the fine bishop's house and into a tiny cottage. Gone were his position and authority. In place of his handsome bishop's salary he received a tiny allowance. As word spread, people sent food and clothes to help his family survive.

If Bunyan Joseph had desired a life of comfort and luxury, he could easily have had it. All he needed to do was sign the papers pressed on him. But he knew it was not the right thing to do, so he would not. He simply went about the work of preaching the gospel and ministering to the poor.

After five years, the British church leader who had been at the heart of the trouble came to see Bunyan Joseph in his thatched cottage. Kneeling before him, the British leader pleaded, "Please forgive me for all you have suffered. We were wrong, and we are sorry."

"There is no need to forgive," Bunyan Joseph answered. "We are one in Christ." The Englishman covered his face and wept.

As Vijayam grew, he attended Christian schools where he was regularly exposed to Bible teaching. He even memorized long passages of Scripture, packing away a great deal of spiritual knowledge in his head. But head knowledge is not heart knowledge, and what was in Vijayam's heart was his little-boy cry: *Look at all the poor people! Where is God's justice?*

As Vijayam approached his teen years, his questions grew sharper and more intense. So what if his family helped the poor? With so much suffering everywhere, with such abject conditions on every side, their paltry actions hardly made a difference.

"So you say God can do anything?" Vijayam challenged his father. "He can miraculously preserve the life of a breech baby? He can send rupees from unexpected places just when they are needed most? Well, then, if God can do all that, why can't he do something about the poverty in this country? And if he can, why doesn't he?"

In his frustration and anger over the gross injustice and suffering all around him, Vijayam turned his back on God and declared himself an atheist. About that time, communist literature began pouring into India. Marxist leaders flocked to schools to rail against the government for its failure to help the poor and to decry the church's pious focus on religion while people starved. "Justice!" they demanded in fiery speeches. "We will have justice in India!"

"Yes! They are exactly right!" Vijayam agreed. "Neither the new national Indian government nor the Christian church is doing anything for the poor. We demand justice!" When it came time to sign up for membership in the communist party, Vijayam was at the head of the line. He worked hard, spoke with burning passion, and quickly moved up to party leadership.

"Anyone who does not become a communist by twenty-one doesn't have a heart." So went an oft-quoted saying in India. "Violent revolution!" insisted the communists. That was the only way to teach a lesson to ruthless landlords who preyed on the poor and took advantage of the helpless. And there is a second half of that saying: "Anyone who remains a communist after twenty-five doesn't have a head."

Vijayam may have been an atheistic leader in the local communist party, but that did not excuse him from morning and evening family worship. Actually, he looked forward to those times. What better opportunity to pelt his father with questions about the existence of God, about salvation, and about God's seeming refusal to intervene on behalf of the poor?

Then one night during family worship, when Vijayam was sixteen years old and in his final year of high school, his father opened the Bible to Colossians 2:13–15: "When you were dead in your sins and in the uncircumcision of your sinful nature, God made you alive with Christ. He forgave us all our sins, having canceled the written code, with its regulations, that was against us and that stood opposed to us; he took it away, nailing it to the cross. And having disarmed the powers and authorities, he made a public spectacle of them, triumphing over them by the cross."

Looking straight at his youngest child—the communist leader, the self-proclaimed atheist with an already hardened heart—Bunyan Joseph said, "You cannot realize you are a sinner and that you would naturally be completely finished. But Jesus took away the consequence of your sins when he nailed the ordinance to the cross on which he died."

Suddenly, it all became blindingly clear: the cross, salvation, the foolishness of all the powers and authorities on earth—and that included communist ideology. The cross had triumphed over them all. All at once it made sense. The answer to the problem of poverty was not anger or hatred, and it never would be. The answer could come only through the love that Jesus demonstrated on the cross. Vijayam fell to his knees and prayed, confessing his sins and begging God's forgiveness.

That night Vijayam couldn't sleep. He had friends living in a Christian hostel, and they were all communists—because of him. It was he, after all, who had persuaded them to join the communist party. As soon as the sun was up, Vijayam was dressed and out the door. He had to tell his friends what happened to him. They had to know that he received new life through Jesus and that he now had joy and an entirely new hope.

At first Vijayam's friends could not understand his new faith. But he wasn't discouraged by their skepticism. Every morning he returned to the hostel to tell them once again the reasons for his faith. Again and again he laid out his explanations. They listened to his words, but what they really noted was the change in his life. In the end, many of his friends also left the communist party to follow Jesus.

※

"You are my portion, O LORD;
I have promised to obey your words. . . . I have considered my
ways and turned my steps to your statutes."
—Psalm 119:57, 59

CHAPTER 2
FOR SUCH A TIME
AS THIS

As they did every Sunday, sixteen-year-old Vijayam and his band of twelve young evangelists set out one blustery afternoon for a village where no one had ever heard of Jesus Christ. Threatening storm clouds gathered in the sky, but the boys, excited about preaching in a new village, ignored them. As they approached the village temple, one fourteen-year-old rushed to the top of the steps and shouted, "The stone idol in this temple is not God! Why do you worship it?"

The infuriated temple priest took an axe in one hand and a sickle in the other and charged toward the boys, shouting that he would chop off their heads. Vijayam stepped forward. "I am willing to die," he said, "but please, would you allow us to pray first?" The startled priest paused as the boys knelt down and began to pray aloud. The priest grabbed Vijayam's hands and pulled him to his feet. "Aren't you afraid of dying?" he asked.

"You are just a boy. I'm sixty years old, and I am terribly afraid to die!"

"Why should I be afraid?" Vijayam answered. "If I die, I will immediately go into the presence of the living God." The priest gasped in amazement. "Never before has anyone said such a thing to me," he said. "Please, tell me more of what you know."

Vijayam began to preach, but the priest stopped him. "Wait! Everyone must hear what you say." The priest called all the people in the village to come, several hundred in all. Then he ordered them to sit and listen to what the young man had to say about the true and living God.

All this time, Vijayam's father was at home praying. As he listened to the pouring rain, he asked God to protect the boys from the fury of the storm. God answered his prayer for protection, but in a way far beyond anything Bunyan Joseph could have imagined.

Since that day Vijayam has made it a habit to begin every day praying and reading God's Word. What lay ahead for him, he could not have imagined. But whatever it was, he knew he could not possibly face it alone. He would definitely need God's power.

God gives gifts to each of us, and Vijayam definitely had a gift for academics. A leader in school, he studied hard and did well. He also played sports well. But Vijayam was still poor. And when it came time for him to take his secondary school examination, he simply did not have the twelve rupees it cost to take the exam. Instead of admitting his plight, he casually announced to his teacher, "I will not be taking the exam. I decided to wait until next year."

Vijayam's teacher was not fooled. He quickly guessed the problem. "This year, I am going to conduct a scholarship examination," he announced to the class. "Whoever stands first will get his secondary school exam free." Vijayam won the competition, and he took the exam.

Vijayam graduated from high school with distinction, scoring the highest marks in the entire district. But his father had no money to send him to college, and colleges catered to families who could afford to pay their fees. Vijayam's parents decided they had no choice but to send their son to a teacher-training school. A small stipend from the government would pay for it.

When Vijayam's oldest brother, Hosea, heard about the training school plans, he decided to take matters into his own hands. Even though Hosea was struggling to stretch his meager salary far enough to care for his own family, he took Vijayam to Madras (now Chennai) to arrange his admission into Madras Christian College. Vijayam's third brother, Azariah, who had failed his own final school examination, went along with them. He hadn't yet mentioned it to anyone, but he had a plan of his own: he would take a job as a salesman for a tea company in Madras.

"Why would you do such a thing?" Hosea demanded when he found out Azariah's plan. "You don't know this city. You don't even speak Tamil!" Azariah responded, "How can you alone support Viji's studies? I will also do my part." Then, the second brother, Abhishekam, who had just received his teacher-training degree, left his pastoral job to work in a school so he, too, could help support his youngest brother's education. "It was the united efforts of my brothers that enabled me to complete my junior college education," Vijayam later said.

At Madras Christian College, Vijayam studied mathematics, physics, and chemistry with the goal of going into engineering. But during one vacation, he happened by a stack of geology books in the library. As he read, an idea dawned on him: *If I were to study geology, I could help my country develop mineral resources, and that would raise the economy.* So, in 1953 he enrolled in graduate studies in geology, with minors in physics and chemistry, at Andhra University in Waltair, in the state of Andhra Pradesh.

In his hostel at Andhra, for the first time in his life Vijayam lived among Hindu students. Every Sunday evening he attended the Union Chapel where he was spiritually nurtured by Canadian Baptist missionaries. Afterward, he went from room to room in the hostel handing out New Testaments. The more Vijayam studied, the more he saw the hand of God in science. He longed to communicate that connection to others, so he began a weekly Bible study where he could meet with other Christian students.

As a member of both the university football and volleyball teams, Vijayam quickly became well known on campus, a situation he considered a divine opportunity to minister. Sometimes he set up loudspeakers outside the campus gate and played Billy Graham messages for everyone to hear. Each Sunday afternoon he held Sunday school for the poor—the scavengers and fishermen who lived next to the university campus. "You're spending far too much time on all this," his friends chided. "You are neglecting your studies." They didn't know that God was preparing Vijayam with more than just an academic education. The young man graduated with honors in 1956, and he did so again the following year when he earned his master's degree.

Vijayam's parents were extremely pleased with the marriage they had arranged between their son Abhishekam and Jayamani, the eldest daughter of M. Gnan Prakasam, a pastor in Kurnool District who was committed to working with the poor and oppressed. They, in fact, were so pleased they approached Jayamani's father and asked if his second daughter, Mary Ravana Chinthamani, could marry their youngest son, Vijayam. Everyone agreed, and the marriage was arranged.

Mary and Vijayam married at Gooty on December 30, 1957. By then, Mary's father had gone to be with the Lord. Since her mother died when she was only two years old, and Mary had spent years caring for her stepmother and three younger brothers, she took Vijayam's parents as her own, and they took her as their daughter.

Years earlier, when little Vijayam gazed over the side of the bullock cart and worried about the suffering poor, God was already preparing a partner for him who would share his concern for the downtrodden. Outspoken, demonstrative, and extremely kind-hearted, Mary is exceedingly tender and sensitive toward those who are hurting and in need. "Mary and I work as a team," Vijayam says. "She understood me right from the beginning. The ministry is for both of us."

Immediately after their wedding, Vijayam began research at Andhra University, and two years later he secured a position with the government as a geologist working in the toughest areas. This meant that Mary spent her newlywed years in jungle tents among tigers, wolves, and snakes. Once, when pregnant, she traveled three days across trackless, unforgiving terrain to visit her husband in a remote jungle area. As they sat and talked in his small tent, they heard noises coming from the kitchen tent behind them. When Vijayam took a torch and opened the door to investigate, a tiger ran out past him and back into the jungle. "I was not always a wise husband," Vijayam said with a note of regret.

In the midst of his research on the black sand beaches of India's east coast peninsula, where the bottom sediments contain radioactive minerals, the Geological Survey of India selected Vijayam as geologist and posted him to Bihar to explore for coal. There, through drilling and exploration, he discovered the thickest coal seam ever found in India.

Success. Wealth. Fame. Finally the doors of possibility were flung wide open. For the Vijayams, everything they could hope for lay within reach—except that these successes were not where their hearts wanted to be. "I could not fulfill my real burden for evangelism," Vijayam explained. And so, in the midst of great success, he and Mary prayed together that God would open up a new career.

When God answers a prayer, he often does so in an unexpected way. Vijayam had prayed for a place to fulfill his calling to evangelize the lost. Well, how about Osmania University in the city of Hyderabad? In his new position as university lecturer, Vijayam was the only Christian on the faculty of two thousand. What better place for a scientist with the heart of an evangelist? The world around him was filled with jealousy, injustice, hatred between castes and religions, cutthroat competition, and rivalry among scientists and researchers. Yet God placed Vijayam in a place where he could let his light shine, pointing them toward God the Father in heaven.

Years later, when Vijayam was selected as professor and chairman of the university's geology department, the vice-chancellor introduced him by saying, "He is Jesus Christ!" Of course, he most certainly is not. Yet that introduction before the audience of Hindus and Muslims gave Vijayam a wonderful opportunity to openly proclaim the truth of who Jesus Christ really is.

During this time Mary worked as a mathematics teacher at Wesley Girls' High School in Secunderabad. A series of miscarriages had caused both Mary and Vijayam great sorrow, but in July 1962 their daughter, Mary Lois Vyjayanthi, was born. Two years later, in September 1964, Rhoda Vidya Sravanthi joined the family. A third daughter, Ruth Lajwanthi, was born in 1967, just as Mary was writing her final thesis for her master's degree in philosophy, which she managed to fit in around her teaching job and mothering. Three beautiful, precious girls, so dear and so loved. Yet the Vijayams still longed for a son. So they prayed and prayed, often into the night. God heard their prayers, and in April 1970 Joseph Vijaywanth was born. Even before his birth, he was dedicated to God for his service.

At Osmania University, God gave Vijayam a special friendship with P. T. George, a lecturer in the Central Institute of English and Foreign Languages. The two began discussing many issues of the Bible. Although George knew the Bible well, he had grave doubts about the uniqueness of Jesus, mainly because of the influence of the teachings of Ramakrishna Paramahamsa. But discuss and argue and explain as he may, Vijayam could not convince his new friend of the truth of Jesus Christ. All he could do was continue to pray for him.

For several years nothing happened. But in time God removed the doubts and questions that plagued George, and he came to believe in Christ. Since then the two men— close friends, counselors, and encouragers—meet often for prayer and fellowship.

On the Osmania campus and also in his home, Vijayam started Bible studies in association with the Union of Evangelical Students of India and Campus Crusade for Christ. Every year, an increasing number of students attended. Still, Vijayam wanted to go outside the college campus. He longed to reach the poor. But how? "Technology!" Vijayam insisted. "Technology for the poor is the bridge. Technology used for God's kingdom."

Rather a unique response, actually. Some people are totally mystified to hear science and evangelism used in the same sentence. For many, the concepts of science and religion just do not go together. "Sometimes I think there is a split in Dr. Vijayam's personality," stated an obviously perplexed young scientist—a former student of Vijayam's who is a secular Hindu from the Brahmin caste. "He is a scientist of the first order, yet he believes in a lot of things that are not scientific. His faith is a contradiction."

That Vijayam is a scientist of the first order is never in dispute. While teaching at Osmania University, he earned his doctoral degree in two years in a branch of geology entirely new to India: sedimentology and petroleum geology. Trained by UNESCO (United Nations Educational, Scientific, and Cultural Organization) in hydrogeology, Vijayam presented papers and taught around the world. He was one of the few Indians selected for a Fulbright scholarship to do postdoctoral research at Northwestern University in Evanston, Illinois, United States, where he mastered the new method of lithofacies contour mapping for oil exploration. Applying contour mapping for the first time and using a new analysis of data, he predicted large reserves of coal, oil, and natural gas on the east coast of India. Since then, all of these have been put to use.

Indians have a saying: "If your relative goes to the U.S., you can bid him a final good-bye. He will not come back to India." Many figured that when the Vijayams got a taste of American life, emigration would be their next step. Surely such a man would go where the good jobs were. Surely he would follow the money. But that's not what happened.

"God gave me the burden to serve India and to spread the gospel among the Indian people," Vijayam said. So in 1966, he returned to India and to his job at the university. He was back home when his mother, Lucy, went to be with the Lord.

While doing research in Chicago, Vijayam had the opportunity to mingle with Christian students at Moody Bible Institute. The contrast he felt back at Osmania University deepened his commitment to raise a strong witness for Christians who work in secular professions. As president of the Fellowship of Professional Workers (FPW) from 1968 to 1984, Vijayam organized a number of residential retreats for professional workers throughout the state of Andhra Pradesh and helped raise funds to build a retreat and training center twelve miles (twenty kilometers) outside the city of Hyderabad. "I was personally much benefited in my spiritual growth by attending these retreats," he said. "It was a great encouragement." Many professional workers committed their lives to the Lord through the efforts of FPW.

So how does a follower of Jesus Christ demonstrate to those around him that he is a disciple of the Master? By working in Christian organizations? Certainly, that does encourage and build up other Christians. By witnessing? That too is vital, although overtly sharing the gospel is not always possible or advisable. Then, by what means? Well, according to Jesus, his disciples are to be marked by their love (see John 13:34–35).

Dr. M. Y. Kamal, a devout Muslim who first met Vijayam when Kamal was a student doing research, found Professor Vijayam to be particularly knowledgeable in his academic area. But that's not what most impressed him. "The most important thing about Vijayam is his love and his deep commitment to this country, this society, the people," said Dr. Kamal. "He could have made his life very comfortable, very luxurious in the U.S. But Vijayam opted to live in India and work for his own people.

He liked to go to the field and work hands-on, to take on the problems of education, literacy, medical care, and a wide variety of things I myself would not know intimately."

Whenever possible, Vijayam spoke of his Christian convictions and the reason for them. Yet he never pushed his opinions on anyone. And despite the fact that some were openly prejudiced against Christians, he was greatly respected on campus. He accepted everyone, whether from a lowly background or a high background. A person did not have to agree with him to gain his respect.

"Science is not against the Bible!" was Vijayam's answer to everyone who questioned the compatibility of science and faith. "It is simply a matter of how we understand the Bible." In the Science and Faith Society he founded, he demonstrated to students and the community just how well faith and science fit together. The scientist with the heart of an evangelist finally got his chance to preach the gospel to the scientific community.

Although Vijayam was careful not to preach in his classes, his Christian character inevitably reflected through his teaching. Off campus he was involved in Christian organizations: Youth for Christ, the Bible Society of India, Gideons International, and Bible Centered Ministries.

Vijayam made no apologies for his spiritual passion, yet he continued to advance in his academic position and influence; and in 1984 he was promoted to chairman of the geology department. But not everyone was pleased about a Christian holding such a high position. One day, as Vijayam was at work in his university office, the door burst open and a group of young men swarmed in, waving knives and yelling threats: "You, Christian! You have no right to hold such a position. We demand you resign! Leave this university at once!"

Shocked, Vijayam looked into the threatening faces glaring at him. He did not recognize any of them. Not one was a student in his classes. "You are against Hindus. You are an enemy of India!" one accused. Another interrupted, "India is for Hindus, not for Christians!" Still another cried, "You are not wanted on this campus!" as he leapt forward and shoved a knife to the professor's throat.

Vijayam's mind whirled. These must be members of a fanatical militant Hindu group. Or perhaps they were students incited by that group. Taking a deep breath, he silently prayed, *God, if this is the day you want me to be in heaven with you, I will rejoice. But, if that is to be, please, take care of my wife and children.*

"You will not leave this room alive!" proclaimed the one threatening Vijayam with a knife. Just as it had when Vijayam was a teenage evangelist standing before the Hindu priest preparing to lop off his head, God's perfect peace swept over Vijayam. For what seemed like hours, he sat in his chair, the knife pressed to his throat.

Then, once again the office door pushed open. This time it was a knot of professors, Hindus all, who crowded inside. They argued and they reasoned and they pacified. They pointed out all that Vijayam had done for the university, for the poor, and for India. "We are Hindus, just like you," they told the militants. "And we are Indians, just like you. Yet we stand fully beside our colleague and friend. If you attack him, you are attacking us."

The militants hesitated. Their bluster faded, and they began to waver. Then, one by one, they backed down.

As he made his way home, Vijayam asked God, "Why did you allow such a thing to happen?" The answer came to him in the words of Matthew 5:11–12: "Blessed are you when people insult you, persecute you and falsely say all kinds of evil against you because of me. Rejoice and be glad because great is your reward in heaven, for in the same way they persecuted the prophets who were before you."

The next day in the vice-chancellor's office, Vijayam offered, "I will resign as department head if you think it best." The vice-chancellor stood up and embraced him. "I know you," he said. "You are good for this university." The vice-chancellor not only refused to accept the resignation but he also gave Vijayam the added responsibility of chairman of the Board of Studies in the university.

"Witness is hardest when people are watching you day after day after day," said Dr. Sanghi, who well remembers that day on campus. "Vijayam was a continual witness, and he made no secret about his faith."

In the end, even the Hindu scientist who could not reconcile science and faith conceded that Vijayam's "faith makes him strong." Then he added, perhaps with a touch of sadness, "It's not that way with me."

The apostle Paul said it this way:

> "But whatever was to my profit I now consider loss for the sake of Christ. What is more, I consider everything

a loss compared to the surpassing greatness of knowing Christ Jesus my Lord, for whose sake I have lost all things. I consider them rubbish, that I may gain Christ and be found in him, not having a righteousness of my own that comes from the law, but that which is through faith in Christ—the righteousness that comes from God and is by faith" (Philippians 3:7–9).

CHAPTER 3
A BETTER
WAY

L akshmi hated her name. Why should she be called "god-dess of wealth" when her little ones cried themselves to sleep every night because the handful of rice she had to give them was not enough to fill their empty stomachs? Sometimes the landowner would offer her a second handful of rice if she stayed behind with him after her husband left for the fields. How she despised the landowner! But when he called to her, she stayed. What choice did she have?

When the Vijayams visited Nandyal, Lakshmi's village, they were shocked at what they saw. Mary had grown up there, and her father was the local pastor; but she had not been back to the area since her wedding. It was a poor village when she was young, so Mary had looked forward to seeing how far it had progressed. But what she found stunned her. Not only had there been no progress, but the people were worse off than ever. Impoverished, brutalized, and exploited for profit, they toiled as virtual slaves in the fields of the local landowner while their children wandered hungry and unsupervised.

A few persistent folks struggled to grow a tiny crop of vegetables to supplement their family's meager diet, but they had little to show for their efforts. The ground was useless and the water supply undependable.

"You need nutrients for the soil," Vijayam explained. "And plants must have water." The villagers mumbled that it wasn't their land. They had no money for soil nutrients, certainly not for land that belonged to someone else. And wasn't it obvious that water was hard to come by?

Vijayam explained, "Equal justice, equitable distribution of wealth and land—these things you cannot accomplish by force. The people themselves must change. And if they are ever to have any power, they must unite." That sounds good. It is extremely difficult, however, to unite the people Gandhi called "Harijans"—outcasts of the Indian social system, now commonly known as Dalits. They've grown used to landlords dominating them, to being told what to do.

To be a Dalit means a life of discrimination, and poverty, and prejudice, and abuse. It means being told every day in countless ways that you are worthless. It means being helpless and hopeless.

As a Dalit, you are relegated the most awful of jobs, such as cleaning sewage pits, scavenging in garbage dumps, or working as bonded slaves in the fields of rich landowners. You pass your slave-like existence on to your children and to your children's children. You are locked in ignorance, because you likely can neither read nor write.

As a Dalit, you are considered inferior, polluted, and sinful—the lowest of the low. You must stay away from the village water well because just your presence will foul the water. Dalits are expected to be Hindus, yet they are banned from entering Hindu temples, even banned from reading Hindu scriptures.

Because this is how Dalits are treated from the day of their birth, most grow up believing not only that they deserve prejudice, mistreatment, and abuse but also that they brought it on themselves by their evil deeds in a former life.

Today, untouchability is outlawed in India, yet it has by no means disappeared. As part of the country's three-thousand-year-old Hindu-based system, it separates Indian society into four main groups, or castes. At the top are Brahmin priests, the elite members of the highest caste. Under Brahmins is the soldier caste, the fighters and defenders. Next in rank are members of the merchant caste, the ones who conduct business and handle money. And then, underneath all the castes is the despised group that for thousands of years was known as "untouchables." These are the Dalits, the "broken people," the "out-castes." Today they make up roughly one-third of India's population. Scheduled tribes, the so-called aboriginal people, are outside the system.

To unite Dalits would be extremely difficult. And yet, extremely difficult does not mean impossible. What if these people were to reach out from their poverty to begin sharing with each other? What if they pooled the few rupees they have and invested the money for the common good of the group? What if, instead of every family scraping by alone, they organized into communities to help each other? What if they were able to build a large enough pool of money to make loans available to the poor at interest rates they could manage? Just imagine if such things were possible.

After all, it's not as if the Dalits have no rights. Basic rights were guaranteed them in the Indian constitution. The Dalits simply had no knowledge of what was due them. And even if they knew, how could they have stood against high caste people of power and influence who could use their money to bribe authorities. If the Dalits, while sweating over their backbreaking labor in landlords' steamy fields, had time to consider such an idea, they would surely have laughed and called it preposterous. For far too long, they had been without a voice and without hope.

Many government and private groups had microenterprise programs in place to benefit the poor, of course. Some were successful, others less so, and some were failures. But Vijayam's thinking led in a different direction. Although Vijayam's heart had always been with the poor, his academic pursuits had crowded in and pushed that passion aside. But in 1975, the Walter Development Society in Hyderabad invited him to start a research institute under its management. He responded by starting Water and Mineral Exploration Research and Training Institute (WAMERTI). As he explored for groundwater to provide drinking water to poverty level villages, his burden for the poor was reborn.

When the Vijayams saw first-hand the villagers of Nandyal, they told the people, "Bonded labor is illegal in this country. You do not have to be slaves to the landowners." When Lakshmi heard this, she slipped back into the shadow of her mud hut. She wondered, *What did these people with their fine clothes and educated talk know of the landowner who controlled her life and the lives of every member of her family?*

Law is law, but reality is reality. Families like Lakshmi's are extremely poor, and they are illiterate. When financial problems come on them, they have nowhere to turn, except to money-lenders, who in most cases just happen to be landowners. Always willing to lend, they charge 60 percent interest. When borrowers cannot make the payments, which they inevitably cannot, the landowners take everything they have, including their small plots of land, and entire families are forced to work until the debts are paid. Unfortunately for the borrowers, the landlords keep all the records, making sure the borrowers can never work off the debt.

After Lakshmi had gathered firewood before dawn, she left with her husband and eleven-year-old daughter to work twelve exhausting hours in the landlord's fields. Beating sun or pouring monsoon rain made no difference. Such workers get just enough time off to eat the small meal allotted them for the day. There is no time to cook or to care for the younger children; the little ones are left in the village to fend for themselves. This harsh and thankless existence is a never-ending cycle of hopelessness as parents like Lakshmi pass their indebtedness to their children and to their children's children.

It was in this unpromising area of chronic drought and despair, in the remote villages of Kurnool district in Andhra Pradesh, that in 1979 the Vijayams helped to start MERIBA (Mission to Encourage Rural Impact in Backward Areas). More than 70 percent of the people in these villages are desperately poor Dalits, and many are Christians. MERIBA means "united body," the perfect name for an organization of fellowships that encourage the downtrodden and oppressed to unite peacefully, to stand together against oppression, and to claim their legal rights under the law. MERIBA gives a voice to people whose cries have gone unheard for centuries.

In ninety target villages, MERIBA organized people like Lakshmi into self-help groups called *sanghams* (fellowships). Through informal education—mostly during nighttime classes—they were taught about the causes of poverty and encouraged to build solidarity and unity. (Later, five similar organizations came together in different parts of Andhra Pradesh state.) In addition, each sangham member brought one rupee every day to put into the group's savings account.

Savings? In an area where a day's pay scarcely buys enough rice to feed a family, where people have never had an extra rupee, where saving for the future is an unknown concept, where the philosophy of karma dictates that everyone is exactly what and where he or she deserves to be, investment in a self-help group is not an easy sell.

Still, a few people did venture forward, especially some of the women. Every day they ate a little less rice so they would have their required rupee to put into the savings account. And after the day's work in the fields was done, they met with Mary and Vijayam to study the alphabet. "Imagine!" they whispered among themselves with growing excitement. "The next time the landlord brings out his scratchings and tells us to approve them with our thumb prints, we will be able to read what he has written. He cannot cheat us anymore!"

In time, first one woman then another said, "I want to pay off my debt to the landlord." Each had the right to apply for a loan from the sangham. What had recently been a ridiculous impossibility now was actually within reach, usually in one to two years. The sangham charged 1 percent interest as opposed to the 60 percent the landlord charged. Why? Because it was not the sangham's goal to make money. The sangham's goal was to see people lifted out of poverty.

The idea of sanghams spread from village to village, allowing more and more people to learn to read and write. But even as the Dalits rejoiced over their accomplishments, many in the higher castes actively opposed what was happening. In one village the landlords were especially angry at the idea of empowering the poor. Mathai, a young man who worked under a landlord, regularly attended the night classes. This infuriated the landlord. He did his best to force Mathai to stop, but the young man refused. One night when Mathai was on his way to class, he was grabbed from behind, forced to the landlord's house, and tied to an electric pole. He was beaten viciously and left unconscious.

The next morning sangham members discovered Mathai still tied to the pole in front of the landlord's house, barely conscious and groaning in pain. They untied the poor boy and carried him to the police station. But even with the evidence bleeding and moaning in front of them, the police refused to take action. They were too afraid of the landlords.

The villagers, however, were unwilling to let the matter drop. They took the young man to Nandyal, headquarters of the administrative region where the magistrate court was in session. There they lodged a complaint, presenting Mathai as evidence. So severely had he been beaten that even then he could not walk on his own. Immediately, the magistrate ordered the arrest of the four members of the landlord's family who were responsible.

But the story did not end there. Once the four were released on bail, they threatened the MERIBA workers for attempting to organize Dalits. When Vijayam, who was president of MERIBA at the time, was informed of the trouble, he and Mary immediately prepared to pack their four children into the jeep and head to the village.

"Don't take your family!" MERIBA workers warned him. "It is far too dangerous!" Putting their trust in God, the Vijayams decided they would all go. After an eight-hour drive, they reached the village. Mathai's father ran to greet Vijayam insisting, "We must teach the landlords a lesson!" But the social workers hastened to caution, saying, "Be very careful! The landlords are extremely angry. They're threatening to throw hand grenades at us."

As Vijayam and his family set out to walk to the village, sangham members poured out to join the procession, all singing loudly. When they approached the section of the village where the landlord lived, Vijayam instructed the people, "Stand in front of his house and speak of the love of God. It is almost Christmas. Talk about the meaning of Christmas and of the Prince of Peace who came into the world."

When the landlords saw the approaching crowd, they braced for angry accusations and violent retaliation. They were certain there would be trouble. But instead they heard words of peace and reconciliation. So impressed were they that two of the guilty men made their way down from the rooftop where they had taken refuge, and they humbly bowed before Vijayam. "Please forgive us," they asked.

"It is not me you have wronged," Vijayam answered. "Here is the father of the one you beat. Will you ask his forgiveness and shake hands with him?" The two paused and looked at the Dalits gathered before them. Untouchables, all. Despised outcasts, every one. Then the two did an amazing thing: they stepped forward and spoke words of humble apology. Yet as amazing as that action was, their next deed was unbelievable—they reached out and took the man's hand in theirs. A gasp arose from the crowd. It was the first time either of the men had ever touched the hand of an untouchable person.

From the beginning, MERIBA has been a grassroots effort. The people may be the poorest of the poor, unable to read and write, and rejected by society; yet this is their movement, and they are in charge of it.

Under the umbrella of MERIBA, sanghams are set up to follow a democratic process. Each sangham has two elected representatives, a man and a woman. Representatives from all the sanghams come together to form the council that meets monthly at the MERIBA headquarters. There they discuss various village concerns, and they consider requests for loans. Every three years the council elects or reelects officers. One female council member stated with more than a little satisfaction, "The next time, we will elect a *woman* president!"

When a sangham member wants to request a loan, he or she submits an application to the local village sangham. Two times each year, each village sangham has an opportunity to present a request to the council, which means that each sangham must choose two from the pile of requests it receives from its members during the year. In the choosing process, highest preference goes to requests for health needs, and second for educational requests. The third highest consideration is for requests that will make the land more usable, such as fertilizer and tools. Then comes discussion over requests for animals, such as goats and water buffaloes. Finally, consideration is given to requests for microbusiness loans. Certain loan requests are not considered at all, such as money for marriage dowries.

Since MERIBA's beginning, over one thousand individual loans have been given, totaling more than eight million rupees. And through all this, not one woman has defaulted on a loan. Not one!

Men are involved in their own sanghams with separate bank accounts, and while not perfect, their repayment rate is also excellent—about 95 percent. Still, when it comes to granting loans, women get preferential treatment. "They are especially

good about record-keeping and making prompt payments," said
P. J. Lawrence, treasurer of MERIBA. "So when a family needs a
loan, the woman is the one who applies." Ironic, is it not? Poor
women, long-neglected, abused, and rejected, are now slowly
gaining financial control in the villages. And how do the men
feel about this? "Happy," Lawrence replied. "Now they are able
to do so much because of the loans their wives get."

The Indian government is now encouraging the sangham
idea as well, although they use the term "savings groups." And
since the MERIBA women have proven themselves to be such
good risks, the government actually helps fund that program.
The government assists in other ways as well. For instance, when
a group saves fifty thousand rupees, maintains regular deposits,
takes out small loans and repays them on schedule, the government responds by offering to match their grants. "Now even the
major banks are coming and saying, 'Why don't you women
take a loan from us?'" said Lawrence with a broad grin. "They see
that these women are a good risk."

Many things have changed since sanghams came to the village. "When I was a child, I did not know one person who ever
went to school," Lakshmi said. "As soon as we could, we went to
work in the fields beside our parents. My daughter was a laborer
from age nine. But no more. Now there are no child laborers in
our village. Now even my girls can go to school."

She paused, almost unable to believe it herself. Then she
continued, "It used to be that we never left our homes. We went
from the fields to the house and back to the fields. Now look
at us. We take the bus to the bank every week. We could go all

the way to Delhi if we wanted. One day, we may even go to America!"

In fact, the Indian government is sending women from MERIBA to other Indian states to share their experiences and ideas with other women. "Someday it will be to all the states of India," Lawrence said. He may well be right. Already a group has gone to Sri Lanka.

As a nongovernmental organization (NGO), MERIBA is required to serve people of all castes, religions, and faiths. The only common denominator is that all are poor. Even so, MERIBA is founded on the Christian principles of caring for each other and doing to others what you would have them do to you. This requires a total change of thinking for many. It is a departure from the traditional Indian approach of karma, which proposes that those who suffer are simply getting what they deserve and paying for the sins of their past life.

It is true that the MERIBA area is strongly Christian. But many people are second or third generation Christians, and the church in the area is not truly committed to the gospel. Although most people in the sanghams are Dalit Christians, the majority are without a strong Christian faith. Many go to church one day and then celebrate a Hindu festival the next. "We start with economic development and empowering the poor," said Mary Vijayam, "then we move on to spiritual development."

"Bring the gospel to Indians in an Indian cup," Sadhu Sundar Singh had admonished. Heeding this advice has raised MERIBA's program far above the programs of other NGOs. For although education is extremely important at MERIBA, they take a nonformal approach to teaching. "We trained people to act out skits and sing songs," Vijayam explained. "Many songs were written right here in this area. Songs, dances, poems, dramas— all these have been used to mobilize people, to raise awareness, and to tell people for what purpose they are uniting."

Certainly, no one needs to tell Dalits that they are oppressed. They are well aware of that fact. What they don't know is that they can take steps to improve their condition. Indeed, if anything is to change for them, they must come together and learn about the rights they already have under India's constitution. Only then will they be in a position to claim those rights. But it is also important that Dalits understand their responsibilities. People must not take the law into their own hands. One person must not take up arms against another person. And ecology is an obligation.

"Through a drama, we present the idea that if there are more forests there will be better rains, therefore better crops and more water," said Vijayam. "There is a very beautiful song about this. As the song is sung, people gather to listen. Once people come, our actors perform the drama."

Although the Indian government is trying to do much for the Dalits, Vijayam said, "Unfortunately, too often their help doesn't reach the people. That's because the people have no idea that they have any benefits coming, nor do they know how to claim the benefits." This is why it is so vital that the people be educated.

Dalits have lived with social injustice for so many centuries that they have come to believe they have no recourse. And unfortunately, this has too often been the case. Because rich landowners have all the power, police and judges have been slow to move against them. But when Dalits come together, when they take action as a unified body and speak with one voice, everything changes.

Oppressors want their victims to feel isolated and alone. They want them to believe they are unprotected and utterly vulnerable. Often the goal is simply to scare people away. And it was easy to do that when everyone stood alone. But now, with sanghams in nearly ninety villages, things are changing.

For instance, a Dalit man had gotten a 30,000-rupee loan from his landlord at a high rate of interest. Even though he had managed to pay back 40,000 rupees several times over, the landlord still took his entire crop as additional payment. Finally, the landlord informed the exasperated Dalit, "You still owe me money, so I will take your land, too." As the Dalit stood helplessly by, the landlord took the deed to the local official to get the land transferred into his name. When the village sangham heard about the situation, they went to the police and reported what was going on. Two months later the court returned the Dalit man's property to him. Then the court reduced his payments to a normal rate—an amount that had long since been paid off, which meant he owed nothing. In addition, the landlord had to repay the man for all the crops he had taken.

Throughout the 1980s the Vijayams were at the forefront of the movement working on behalf of bonded laborers—one family at a time, one village at a time. For despite the well-intentioned government laws, poor laborers continued to be paid exceedingly paltry wages. They had no savings, and no credit facilities were available to them. Poverty, sickness, and marriage forced them to borrow from the landlords, their only source of money. So the illiterate borrowers continued to mortgage their lands and sign loans at ridiculously high interest rates they could never possibly pay. And they continued to live and die in bondage, passing their indebtedness to the next generation, and to the next, and the next.

A similar system of oppression is recorded in Nehemiah 5:1–5. That situation made Nehemiah so angry that he called a large gathering of people together to stop it. By applying Nehemiah's method through ACHOR (Action to Conscientize, Humanize, and Organize Rural Poor), an NGO engaged in the liberation of bonded laborers, the Vijayams organized poor laborers to action.

For ten years Mary Vijayam served as chairperson of ACHOR. She and Vijayam worked with the laborers, going to the villages at night when their own children were sleeping or sometimes taking their little ones along with them. Their approach was to hold a meeting in the villages of bonded laborers, teach the villagers songs, and then, when all were gathered together, explain to the people their rights under Indian law.

The Vijayams would build a small community house in the village where they could meet and hold basic literacy classes to teach the alphabet, how to sign one's name, and how to read bus numbers. They would also give much-needed instruction in hygiene and health care. And they would show the people how to grow a kitchen garden so that, even on a small piece of land, a family could grow nutritious food and have some income.

Villagers were encouraged to get a water buffalo that would provide milk and milk products, both for their own children to drink and as a product to sell. Also, families could sell the calves. The end goal was to enable mothers to earn enough money to stay home and care for their children.

Empowerment —what a wonderful goal! Wonderful, that is, for everyone except the landowners. Suddenly, no one was willing to work their fields at slave wages. People once securely under their control no longer obeyed their orders. For the landowners, empowering the Dalits was a bad thing. And they did not accept it easily.

In 1981, near the village of Dayara, close to Ghatkesar, the Vijayams spoke to a crowd of three hundred sangham members until late at night. As Vijayam's voice echoed over the loudspeaker, the entire village gathered to listen, including the landlords. And the more the landlords heard, the more incensed they grew. How dare the Vijayams organize the poor to resist exploitation!

As the Vijayams prepared to return home that night, several sangham members sensed danger, so they also got into the jeep and rode along. When the Vijayams felt they were a safe enough distance from the village, they persuaded the villagers to go back home. The Vijayams continued on their way, following the cart track through the jungle. But as the jeep cleared a rise, they found themselves headed straight for a crowd of about twenty people, armed with clubs and sticks, blocking their way.

"We dare not stop," the terrified driver warned. "If we do, they will surely beat us up or worse." Immediately, the Vijayams began to pray. Then, trusting the Lord, Vijayam told the driver, "Rev up the engine, and drive on." The driver did. And the mob parted, making way for the jeep. No one was injured, not the Vijayams and not one of the would-be attackers.

The next morning the Vijayams answered the knock at their door to find a group of badly beaten villagers, cut and bruised. The landlords, in their frustration, had turned their thugs on the people of the village. But if the intention was to intimidate the people, the landlords had failed. For the actual result was a village more unified and more determined than ever to stand up to their exploiters.

In the sun-drenched heat of summer, when the west winds blow, newly freed laborers of one Christian Dalit village began their day as usual. When the landowner constructed this particular village, he encircled the compound of two hundred thatched-roof huts with haystacks. This particular morning, as winds blew strong, the men and women set out for the fields to harvest the crops, leaving the children and old people at home. The landlord saw his chance. Creeping in, he set the dry haystacks on fire. Immediately, flames roared up and enveloped the village. Assuming his most innocent look, the landlord shook his head and murmured, "Too bad, too bad. But accidents will happen." As the smoke grew thick, the men and women in the fields saw it and rushed back to their homes. But they were too late. Everything was gone. So was the landlord.

When the Vijayams got word of the tragedy, Mary quickly collected clothes for the women and children and gathered food to take to the village. The Vijayams arrived to find stunned people milling around among the ashes in the scorching summer sun. Quickly, Mary ordered tents to be put up to provide shelter.

"Come and pray for us!" the people begged. Shocked by the devastation, Vijayam made his way from one pile of ashes to another to pray.

"I didn't know what to do," he said, "so I said to the people, 'Let's all pray.' They asked me to speak, but I told them I didn't have any words. I suggested we sing a song."

A boy of about sixteen said he had composed a song to sing on Good Friday, which was the very next day. The chorus was "My house also is not my own, the only thing on which I have faith is the way to the cross of Jesus." In a clear, strong voice, the boy sang his song, and whenever he came to the chorus, everyone joined in. He was singing, people were crying, an old lady started praying, then another, and another. "Fire can destroy our homes but not our faith," Vijayam told the people. And all this time Mary was busying herself unloading the rice she brought, knowing it would be several hours before there was food cooked for the hungry villagers.

Suddenly, a big bullock cart filled with pots of rice and vegetables, cooked and ready to eat, came rumbling down the road. The villagers stopped their singing. "What is this?" they called out. "Where are you coming from?"

"Oh, we belong to the village a few kilometers down the road," the new people said. "We saw the smoke, and we guessed what happened. So we gathered the rice and food we had prepared for our own dinners, and we brought it for you."

It was a gift of love from one poverty-stricken village to another, needy Christians giving sacrificially to other Christians they didn't even know but who were in greater need. And together, in the midst of the ashes, brothers and sisters in Christ were praising God.

❦

"In everything I did, I showed you that by this kind of hard work we must help the weak, remembering the words the Lord Jesus himself said: 'It is more blessed to give than to receive.'"

—Acts 20:35

CHAPTER 4
IF NOT I,
THEN WHO?

At 8:30 in the morning a young Hindu student knocked nervously on Dr. Vijayam's office door at Osmania University. He was eager to meet the popular professor. Perhaps if he were fortunate, he might even secure a job with him. But the student had arrived too late. Dr. Vijayam was already gone, having left for a day of fieldwork. Hours from home and desperate for the job, the student decided to wait around and hope for an appointment for the following day. When he returned at 5:30 in the afternoon, instead of an appointment waiting for him, he met Dr. Vijayam himself.

"I never thought a man who had been working in the field all day out in the hot sun would have time for me," said Dr. Mani, now a respected scientist himself, as he looked back on that day. "But he welcomed me and asked me all about myself."

It was 1977, the year best remembered for a catastrophic cyclone followed by a tsunami on India's east coast, near the

Krisna River delta. Reports were just beginning to pour in: as many as 200,000 people were dead, and the destruction was terrible. A deluge of salty sea water left the entire area without fresh water to drink.

"I'm putting a team together," Dr. Vijayam told the young man in his office. "Hydrogeologists, geophysicists, sociologists, and social workers. We'll help with relief work, but our main job will be to get fresh drinking water to the survivors. I need someone with your skills. Will you join us?"

The student hesitated. He had no confidence that he could actually do such a job. And yet, how could he waste such an opportunity? So, with more than a few qualms, he managed to stammer an unsteady "Yes, Sir."

In the cyclone-affected area, the team of ten gasped at the sight of piles of dead bodies, all preserved by the salt. "They were everywhere," Mani recalled. "You would walk along and accidentally step on somebody." Then the team headed to the villages where they were surrounded by people begging for fresh water. "I'd never seen anything like it. But I tried to follow Vijayam's leading and talk to the people, sympathize with them for their problems, and give as much as I could."

While the cyclone changed Mani's life, it was also a turning point for Vijayam. At the time, he was serving with WAMERTI, working in the villages among the poorest of India's people. But as he saw this desperation for water, he realized that he could do much more. First, he must take a fresh look at Rural Development and Advisory Services (RDAS), the NGO social action group in which he played a major part. As the only physical scientist among the group of social scientists, he could see first hand that such organizations were handicapped in their holistic approach to development because they could not fully understand how science, technology, and income-generating activities could help the poor.

"There needs to be more than just social organization," Vijayam insisted. "There should also be a transfer of contextual technology. It should be reaching the poor. Often we scientists tend to keep scientific knowledge to ourselves and not make it available to those who are really in need. Nehru, India's first prime minister, said, 'Scientists in India should not be in their ivory towers. They should come down to the grassroots level.'"

In the summer of 1982, RDAS organized a seminar for volunteer organizations, donor agencies, and government departments. On the final day Vijayam had the privilege of addressing the entire association. "Do you know how a small farmer outside the fence of your institution is working with his land?" he asked. The scientists in the room admitted they did not. "Do you have any desire to find out?" Vijayam pressed. They said they did, but that they just did not have time. They were too busy doing important research to pursue such things.

"No!" Vijayam insisted. "A scientist *must* learn from the people." Then he proposed the idea of a voluntary association through which scientists could use their expertise to help the poor. And he offered this challenge: "Every Saturday is a free day for us. In addition, we have eighteen public holidays. Altogether you are free about 150 days in the year. Can you take one-tenth of that time to go to visit a village? Maybe ten or fifteen days in the entire year? If you will agree to do this, we will even provide you with transportation."

By the next morning three donor agencies had approached Vijayam to ask how they might get involved. PROGRESS had begun.

PROGRESS (Peoples Research Organization for Grass Root Environmental Scientific Services), officially organized in 1983, is dedicated to the progressive development of the poorest among India's rural poor. The staff, governing body, and alumni are leading scientists, sociologists, academics, and university researchers, all committed to a holistic approach of alleviating poverty and providing the poor with sustainable development. Lofty goals indeed, but not surprising. From the beginning, PROGRESS has been innovative in its approach and bold in its vision. And this voluntary association of scientists is literally transforming the future for India's poor.

When bonded labor was abolished in her village and in the villages around her, Lakshmi, like each of the other laborers released, collected five hundred rupees from the government as stipulated in India's Bonded Labor Act. Within a couple of months, like each of the other recipients, she was also given five thousand rupees to enable her to stand on her own. PROGRESS workers were on hand to advise Lakshmi and the other villagers on ways they could put their money to profitable use.

Many of the newly released people were trained in agriculture, so it was natural that they pursue farming. Some opened small shops, such as a shoe repair shop. Lakshmi and several other women learned to raise a herd of specially bred dairy cows. Today the once helpless and hopeless villages are self-sufficient and independent. Older people cannot believe it is actually happening. The younger generation, raised with education and empowerment, will never know a time when society didn't include their voice.

If we compare money, prestige, security, and the exalted life of a professor with humility, dependence on God, and advocacy for the poorest of the poor, some people may think it strange that Vijayam chose the latter course. It seems less strange, however, when considering that the Bible, his ultimate guide, states, "He has showed you, O man, what is good. And what does the LORD require of you? To act justly and to love mercy and to walk humbly with your God" (Micah 6:8).

"The gospel needs to be the holistic gospel," Vijayam insists. "As the Bible says, it is no use telling a person who is naked and hungry to go in peace without actually taking care of that person's physical needs. If oppressed people are deprived by our government of many of the facilities our constitution made available, could it be that the people who are experienced at getting those benefits to the poor are themselves exploiters? That they are not really concerned socially as long as they make a profit? Scientists thought they were good people, and it is true that they have done a lot of good scientific research. But part of that research should be contextualized for the conditions in which the poor live. That's why I thought scientists should become volunteers in such technological needs."

To succeed in such an endeavor would take a work of God. Yet, from his early years Vijayam had witnessed the hand of God at work.

From its inception PROGRESS has advocated on behalf of the poorest of the poor—the Dalits. At the request of the Indian government, Vijayam conducted an evaluation of one district in South India that included people in four states. Through surveys of both families and natural resources—soil, water, land, agriculture, small industries, and women's concerns and psychological issues—PROGRESS came up with a five-year plan. The development should not be at a political boundary, the report determined, but rather at a natural boundary, such as a watershed. The government accepted the plan, including the structural importance of the people—it was they who were to make the actual decisions. Scientists would only offer a cafeteria of ideas so the people would have a choice.

First and foremost, PROGRESS is an advisory organization. Through *action research*—research that can be put into practice by even the most marginalized, small-plot farmer, who then shares the resource with others—PROGRESS has provided to local sanghams, such as MERIBA and government organizations, the scientific know-how and technology to empower, train, and equip India's poor.

In one village the people had problems keeping their dairy cows out of their fields. "You solve this yourselves," Vijayam told the people. When he returned to the village, he saw they had done exactly that. They had started building a rock fence around their fields. When they ran short of equipment, they took out a loan of 1,500 rupees, and the fence was to be completed by the end of the year.

"When it is finished, write to us, and I'll bring scientists here," Vijayam told the villagers. "They will advise you what you can start doing next June or July to prepare for the next season's crops." Advice and guidance that enables the people to help themselves is real progress!

PROGRESS owns no land and has no assets, a difficult situation for an organization that depends on land-based models. But other programs founded by Vijayam—TENT and IWILL—also benefit greatly from the PROGRESS models. TENT purchased seven and one-half acres of land for the express purpose of establishing a model farm. (Now the farm has expanded to almost twelve acres.) Today, lush acres developed, planted, and overseen by three scientists make up a good part of the farm. These three men have been part of the project since the beginning—B. V. Rama Rao, professor of horticulture; A. Hanumantha Rao, professor of agriculture; and S. Sethuram, professor of animal husbandry.

India's governmental Department of Science and Technology's division of Science and Society allows the government to provide money to individuals who are doing work on behalf of the poor and marginalized. The Land Ceiling Act, under the Ministry of Environment and Forest, also helps. When Indira Gandhi was prime minister of India, she ordered that excess land, "over the ceiling" of a certain amount, be taken from rich farmers and released to landless people. These lands, however, have poor soil and no water, and they are rocky and highly sloped. Nothing can grow on such land. Dalit families did indeed receive about a half acre of land, but what could they do with it? The land was useless.

"We approached the Ministry, and they gave us finances," Vijayam said. "Once the land is in the hands of the people, MERIBA organizes them into a sangham, and they learn to share. Then PROGRESS comes in with science and technology interventions." And because it directly benefits the poorest of the poor, PROGRESS was able to apply for funding through the Science and Society division. Today, the Indian government is the total financial support for the program.

"Change will take time, but through PROGRESS we are finally moving toward it," said a young social worker participating in the program. "The next generation will definitely see a difference."

✃

"So neither he who plants nor he who waters is anything, but only God, who makes things grow."
—1 Corinthians 3:7

CHAPTER 5
TRANSCENDING
DIVIDES

I ndia. A land teeming with 1.1 billion people in a country one-third the size of the United States—16 percent of the world's population living on 2.5 percent of its land. A difficult concept for the West to grasp, especially Americans. Vijayam explained it this way: "If everyone from Canada moved down into the United States, then if the entire population of the continent of Africa poured in on top of them, and then if all those people were squeezed over into the states west of the Rocky Mountains, you would have an approximation of the population concentration in India. And every year that population grows by the number of people in the continent of Australia."

Within India are divisions of mind-boggling proportions, seemingly unbridgeable chasms. A privileged high caste versus rejected untouchables. Select, upwardly mobile individuals versus starvation-poor masses. The educated elite versus the illiterate majority. Hindus versus Christians versus Muslims. Nuclear power versus plodding, third-world ox carts.

The university world where Vijayam spent his days was filled with Hindus from the highly educated, top level of Indian society. His evening and weekend work with PROGRESS mainly involved the poor, downtrodden, and illiterate. And around these two, he remained active with organizations that drew in the tiny Christian minority.

Perhaps this diversity in his own life allowed Vijayam to recruit young, eager professionals and well-respected scientists to assist in PROGRESS without concerning himself with how to bridge the obvious social divides. The success of PROGRESS owes a great deal to the young professionals who, while they do receive a stipend for their work, are paid much less than they would receive in a university or industry position. All highly qualified, they make a financial sacrifice to work with the organization.

Why do they do it? One young scientist answered, "We were brought up in cities. We are from the high life. But after seeing the poor, we want to help them come up in life. We do want to live the good life, but we want to be among these others to help see that they have a future, too."

An older scientist who has worked with PROGRESS for many years explained it this way: "When I worked with the government, I only went to the rich people, to the landlords. They accept the new technology. But it was a whole new experience to go to the poorest of the poor, to understand their problems, and to do something to help their situation. They suffer from many diseases, but they can grow things in their own backyards that will improve their health and their life if someone just teaches them how to do it."

"All we learned in the university was theory," a social worker added. "But here I am gaining practical experience for what I really want to do in life. It is a two-way benefit."

Actually, it's a three-way benefit. PROGRESS is also contributing to the well-being of the entire country of India. In the twenty years PROGRESS has been in existence, over 180 scientists from a number of disciplines have passed through the program. Many are now in high positions, either with the Indian government or in multinational companies in India, such as the World Bank. And it is true that these scientists do indeed gain as well as give. The first three to join—Hanumantha Rao, Rama Rao, and Sethuram—were exactly of the caliber Vijayam had in mind for the project. Now in their late 70s and early 80s, all three are still with the organization and have trained hundreds of people.

"When we give technology to the poor, they can assert themselves and make themselves equal with the rest. That is what PROGRESS does," explained Vijayam. "The scientists are Hindus and people of higher caste, yet they have a vision of bringing up the lower castes, so we have a common goal."

Hanumantha Rao, who has a master's degree from Kansas State University, is an agronomist who specialized in grassland management. He had just retired from the university when he received a call from Vijayam asking him to help at PROGRESS.

At the time, Hanumantha Rao, a Hindu, was working with Christian missionaries. "That was fortunate for me," he recalled, "because Christian missionaries are devoted, and they are sincere and honest." Still, before PROGRESS he had never been in contact with a poor person. His only contact was with rich farmers. Yet he was immediately interested in the position. "I'm an agronomist," he said. "How to utilize the land, how to best make the soil retain the water to make the plants grow . . . I had gained so much knowledge over the years, I did not want to waste it." And then he added, "I do not discriminate. People are people . . . we should all treat them as that."

A secular organization, PROGRESS has been especially successful at bridging India's deep social chasms of caste, religion, education, gender, and socio-economic status. And the common link across the divides has been technology. "Technology is needed for a caste-free community," Hanumantha Rao insisted. "Many of the Hindus are in favor of working together for the good of the country. The poorest of the poor need so many programs, but so far all the programs have been reaching the richer sections of society. Eighty percent of the poor have only 20 percent of the resources."

Rama Rao had been a professor of horticulture for thirty-five years when he read a newspaper ad asking for scientists to work with PROGESS. "I wanted some activity, so I decided to apply for it," he said. It just so happened that Rama Rao was a friend and colleague of Hanumantha Rao, who was the one reviewing applicants for the position. Imagine Hanumantha Rao's amazement when he saw his friend's name on the application.

Although he hoped they could work together, he decided that to be fair he really should remove himself from the interview. Even so, Rama Rao was selected, and the two have worked closely ever since. "We are much in contact with the poor people," says Rama Rao. "The actual work is in the field with the poorest of the poor."

"If we had stayed in the university community or the private sector, we could have made a lot of money," acknowledged Hanumantha Rao. "A *lot* of money! But we are far richer this way. We have the love and affection of the people. We see our investment in people, not in money."

Rama Rao agreed. "We have an interest to work with the very poorest of the poor people. And all our projects are aimed at their development. Tremendous things have happened through PROGRESS. It is truly fantastic. Remarkable! Some of the programs are particularly meant for women. Sharing of resources helps the poorest of the poor, with the emphasis on the women. That is something marvelous. Just marvelous!"

His enthusiasm bubbling, Rama Rao told of ten women involved in a PROGRESS project that mixes farming and crop production. With ten original cross-bred cows, the women raised the fodder on two and one-half hectares of land using water in an especially efficient way. The women were asked how they thought the program had benefited them, Rama Rao recalled, and he quoted their answer: "It is a wonderful program. Our children's health is very good. They drink cow's milk, which they never had before." Then, he said, the women added with pride, "We even know how to raise the fodder ourselves!"

Hanumantha Rao smiled as he remembered the difficulties they had getting the women to try new things. "We said 'crossbreed,' and they said, 'No, we never raised these other kind of cows. We are already profitable.' We brought the women to see the model farm. It took us almost a year and a half to convince them to take the cross-bred cows!"

"At first the government paid money to support the women," Hanumantha Rao said. "But now the women are on their own. They get loans locally from their own bank—a bank they established! It is fantastic. They have their own building, their own school, their own land. Can you imagine? It is absolutely fantastic!"

Poverty-level Dalit women in business—and on their own land, at that. Securing loans from the bank. Even running their own bank. Illiterate women establishing schools for children who cannot meet the basic requirements for enrollment in public schools. Yes, it is fantastic indeed!

PROGRESS is now working in sixty villages in central India. The programs are inspected by the government of India, since the government is providing so many of the loans. No waste. No misappropriation. Institutions working on their own research translated to the good of the poorest of the poor. What the government looks for is a connection between the scientist and the poor people, and that is exactly what the government finds.

"It is very satisfying," said Hanumantha Rao. "The technology here is second to none, but the crucial issue is how it is transferred to the poor. Otherwise, the country will remain just as it is. Otherwise nothing will change for India."

Look at the impressive array of PROGRESS models in contextual technology:

- **Water:** This is the single greatest need of the poor. Water management, soil conservation, groundwater exploration, water wells, and crop irrigation are just part of this expansive model.

- **Agriculture:** This important area includes organic farming, best use of limited-use land, dry farming, and alternative farming methods such as mushroom production.

- **Horticulture:** Vegetable farms, kitchen gardens, medicinal plants, dry-land horticulture—all this and much more is involved in this vital area.

- **Forestry:** Besides farm and social forestry, reforestation is an important element here.

- **Animal Husbandry:** This area includes dairying, pastoral farming, and raising lambs, poultry, rabbits, or fish.

- **Women's Industries:** Landless women are able to be involved in all of the programs. In addition, they learn fruit processing and preservation, garment making, soap and candle making, handicraft making, and various microenterprises that result in self-sufficiency.

- **Rural Industries and Marketing:** This model includes a variety of options such as making leather products or pottery, quarrying, producing organic pesticides and fertilizers, vermi-composting from worms, and producing blue-green algae that vastly increases the productivity of crops.

Ask Vijayam about PROGRESS and he will excitedly talk as long as you are willing to listen. Get him started on stories of people whose lives have been transformed, and you had better make yourself comfortable, because it will take awhile. But Vijayam does not like attention focused on him, even though his work and accomplishments have earned wide praise, including the prestigious Scientist of the Year Award from the Indian National Science Academy in 1995. Ask him about that award and Vijayam will simply say, "God has used me as a scientist in the field of water exploration and management. He has also seen fit to use me to mobilize voluntary efforts by scientists in this country to the development of the poor. It is so encouraging to see the people participate in developing themselves."

Pivotal points in history have often turned on the efforts of a single person who seized the potential of the moment. God used those people in their particular area of expertise, and their accomplishment rallied those around them to action. This is true about ordinary folks such as Moses and Queen Esther in the Bible, Nelson Mandela in South Africa, and Martin Luther King in the United States. Not one of them set out to change the world. They simply saw injustice, and they determined they could not . . . would not . . . look away and let it pass.

Yet for every one of these celebrated people, countless others—such as Vijayam—have quietly made a similar choice in their own corner of the world. They would not sit by, wishing things were different. They, too, refused to simply shrug and say, "Well, what can one person do?" They spoke out, they acted, and they used the ability God gave them in the place where God put them. And in thousands of places, through the efforts of thousands of everyday people, lives have been changed.

This work is not about Vijayam—it reaches far beyond him. "Vijayam is a great scientist," said Rama Rao. "It is our privilege to work with him. But the great thing is [that] PROGRESS will keep on growing. It will outlive us all." And yet, such a movement requires the efforts of a person who is willing to seize the moment.

"He is an evangelist, he is a scientist, he is a sociologist," said Hanumantha Rao (a Hindu) of Vijayam. "So he can interact and mingle with any of these."

Dr. Kamal, a Muslim scientist who was once a student of Dr. Vijayam and is now involved with PROGRESS, said, "His main aim is to help the poor. And in the process, he welcomes all kinds of people who come to him. Dr. Vijayam's philosophy is that he will help people, and he expects those people to help others in turn."

And the work Vijayam does so faithfully gives credibility to the faith he confesses. "It is good to see someone working across the lines of caste and religion," one young bio-chemist working with PROGRESS observed. "Religion should never stand in the way of doing the right thing. When you look at PROGRESS, you see all creeds, all castes, all religions. We Indians are united at last. At last we are working together toward saving our country."

Because his strong personal concern for the poor is evident to everyone working with him, Vijayam spreads that concern to others who may not naturally share it—Dr. Mani, for instance. For many years the groundwater scientist with PROGRESS, Dr. Mani was among the first on the scene after a devastating earthquake in 1993. "I don't think I had that concern before I went with Dr. Vijayam after the disaster. But what I did out in the villages back then, I'm replicating today. And it will be a part of the rest of my life because anything I do will be defined by that experience. Wherever I am, I'm taking with me the same kind of concern I learned from him."

Well, not exactly the same. Because while many social chasms are being bridged, Vijayam makes no secret of the fact that his faith is the motivating factor behind his actions. While he doesn't preach to those with whom he works, neither does he hide the fact that he is a follower of Jesus Christ. And for many, this is a point of wonder.

Hinduism is inclusive—not when it comes to matters of caste, of course, but spiritually it is an open-minded philosophy. Christ is God incarnate? No problem. Many Hindus believe that the great god Vishnu has had many incarnations, so why not accept Jesus as one of them? The rub comes when Christians claim that Jesus is *the* way, *the* truth, and *the* life—the *only* way to God. They claim that the God of the Bible is the one true God, and there is no other. This is why Vijayam does not depend on words and arguments. Rather, he shows the love of the true God by following Christ's example in his treatment of society's most vulnerable members, by demonstrating in his deeds that they, too, are dearly loved by God.

"If you love something, it should be practiced, not just preached," said Hanumantha Rao. Those words are true of science and technology. But they are even truer when used in the context of God's love and grace. "When I see what is being done in PROGRESS," one Hindu scientist observed, "it makes me wonder why I am not a Christian myself."

∾

"What good is it, my brothers, if a man claims to have faith but
has no deeds? Can such faith save him? Suppose a brother or
sister is without clothes and daily food. If one of you
says to him, 'Go, I wish you well; keep warm and well fed,'
but does nothing about his physical needs, what good is it?
In the same way, faith by itself, if it is not accompanied by
action, is dead. But someone will say, 'You have faith;
I have deeds.' Show me your faith without deeds,
and I will show you my faith by what I do."
—James 2:14–18

CHAPTER 6

A GENERATION CHANGING

N o one rejoiced on the day Ratna was born. Her father grunted in disgust and turned away. A girl! Another financial burden he would have to bear, and then he would be required to pay a huge dowry to get her married. He wanted to take her to the river, throw her in, and rid the family of the curse. Ratna's mother kept quiet. She couldn't help but wonder if it might not be better to let her husband have his way than to condemn her baby daughter to grow up a poor Dalit, forever indebted to a landowner. It was Ratna's grandmother, her father's mother, who said, "No, let the baby live. We need someone to clean the house and care for the sons you will have."

So Ratna lived to work and go hungry, to work and be given in marriage to an old man who did not require much of a dowry, to work and bear children, to work, and work, and work.

But Ratna also lived to see change. When her husband died, she was not forced into the streets to beg. She had learned to read and write in classes the Vijayams taught, and she was able to get a loan to grow mango trees specially developed at PROGRESS for fast growth, high yield, and easy picking. She built a business and created jobs for other women who picked the fruit and carried it to the market. Her children went to school, and she found a good husband for her daughter.

Who could have known? Ratna, who was almost drowned the day she was born, lived to see her generation changing.

So what exactly does "a generation of change" mean? It means empowerment, basic rights, and power through unity. It means being heard respectfully and reaching out in kindness. It means continuing on.

Empowerment

When the women of one village applied for a loan to buy two water buffaloes, they had a plan: all the village women would own the animals together. After working in the fields all day, the women would take turns cutting grass along the side of the road in the evening and carrying it on their head to the buffalo enclosure the men had worked together to build. Great plan, but unfortunately problems quickly arose. Higher-caste people who lived on the other side of the village complained, saying, "The roads are in our area of the village, so that grass belongs to us!"

None of the women owned land. They did, however, have hungry buffaloes that needed to be fed. So they turned to the only other source of fodder they knew—the grass that grew alongside the landlords' fields. That worked for a short time. But as soon as the landlords saw what the women were doing, they, too, ordered them to stop: "You are not permitted to take anything that grows near our fields!"

Without grass, the two buffaloes would starve. On the other hand, without laborers to pick the crops, the landlords' fields would not be harvested. So the wise village laborers said, "As long as we are not allowed to cut the grass on the road beside your fields for our buffaloes, we will not do any work in your fields."

True to their word, not one worker went to the fields to work that day. Again the next day, no workers. The landlords looked at their fields, ripe and ready to be harvested, and fear rose within them. When no workers came on the third day, the panicked landlords exclaimed, "All right! Help yourself to the grass on the road. In fact, go ahead and glean from the fields as well. Take whatever you need. But, please, just come back to work!"

Basic Rights

Access to water is an ever-present concern throughout India. In one drought-prone region, the government had established a well on each side of one village to make certain no one in the area lacked water. The first well was located in the mostly high caste area, while the other was in the poor, Dalit section. When the well in the Dalit area dried up, a Dalit boy carried his water jug to the first well and began to draw water. Immediately, a group of high caste people rushed over and shoved him away. "How dare you draw water from *our* well!" they demanded. When the boy tried to go back to get his water jar, the high caste villagers grabbed sticks and beat him away. In terror, the little boy ran off.

The high caste villagers figured that would end the matter. In the past, thirsty Dalits had always scrounged the ditches for water. Why should this time be different?

But this time was different. Peacefully but firmly, the Dalits went together to their government official and presented the situation. Because they were united as a group, and because the law was on their side, the officials had no choice but to listen. Today, both wells are completely accessible to everyone in the village, regardless of caste.

Power through Unity

In another village a group of higher caste men armed with clubs blocked a bullock cart carrying four Dalit teenagers. The men pulled one boy out of the cart and beat him. "That's what you get for stealing from our house!" they cried as they hit him again and again.

The next day, when the council called a meeting to address the matter, nearly one hundred people from several villages showed up to express their outrage. "Those men have no right to decide whether that boy is innocent or guilty," they protested. "It is a matter for the police to determine, not them!"

Then, as a group, they headed for the police station. "Those men tied up the boy and beat him, although there is no reason to think he is guilty of anything," the head of the sangham stated. "We insist that you arrest them."

The police officers looked at each other. Arrest high caste people of power? Just because they beat a Dalit boy? The policemen shrugged and went back to work. But the Dalit spokesman insisted, "If you are not going to arrest them, we will go to your superior. You are not upholding the law. We insist you do your duty."

When it became apparent that one hundred villagers who knew their rights were not going to give up until justice was done, the police were forced to arrest the aggressors and take them to a court of law. There they were found guilty and punished.

"We used to be barred from the government," one woman said in wonder. "But now our voices are heard. We go to the police for justice, and they do not shut us out. They say, 'Come! We want to help you!'"

Being Heard Respectfully

When a young Dalit named Deva decided to start a tailoring business, he chose a most unlikely partner—his former landlord. With the five-hundred-rupee loan he got from his sangham, he set up shop in the landlord's building. Unfortunately, the landlord did not grasp the meaning of "partners." Whenever anything displeased him, he responded by grabbing a stick and beating the young man. After one especially severe beating, Deva decided he'd had enough, so he went to his village sangham and pleaded for help. The sangham went to the council, and the council went to the Dalit people. Battered and limping, Deva approached the police station to file a complaint, but he did not go alone. As the landlord gazed over the crowd of Dalits that accompanied Deva, he grew more and more alarmed. "Let us not be hasty now," the landlord said to Deva. "Surely we can work this out."

And they did. The landlord gave himself up to the police, who promptly arrested him and put him in jail. The sangham met and put together a compromise. When the landlord heard the terms, he readily agreed to every one of them. He also apologized profusely for his actions, not only to the young man but also to the entire sangham.

"We discussed the situation as equals," one of the Dalit villagers marveled, "the police and the landlord and us. We worked it out together . . . just like equals!"

Reaching Out in Kindness

Like most rural villages, one in which an early sangham formed had only one well. Most of the time it provided sufficient water for everyone, but whenever a drought came, as it periodically did, water was scarce and all the crops died. So the sangham members went to the other villagers and suggested they work together to construct a second well. The other villagers looked out at the pouring rain. Then they looked at the fields, filled with tall, green crops. And laughing aloud, they turned and walked away. So the sangham members dug the well alone. They also paid all the costs. And all the while, the other villagers mocked the foolishness of their neighbors.

But then the rains stopped. Before long, crops began to dry in the fields and turn brown—all crops except those belonging to sangham members, that is. Because their well was flowing just fine, their water jars continued to be filled, and their crops remained as lush as ever.

"Share your water with us," the other villagers pleaded as the situation became more desperate. Share water with neighbors who refused to help pay for the well? Who laughed and ridiculed as the sangham members worked? Why should they share their water?

Yet, parched crops were dying in the fields next to theirs. When the sangham members looked at their thirsty, anguished neighbors, it was through eyes of compassion rather than through eyes of karma. Asking nothing in return, they stepped aside and welcomed their neighbors to help themselves to the water. Because of this kindness, the number of sangham members in that village immediately jumped from 72 to 120.

Continuing On

There is still a long way to go in this process. The wealthy are used to having things their own way, and they will not easily relinquish their positions of power. But a generation changing means that a generation is learning to make its own way.

For example, a controversy arose before a big, three-day meeting, intended to include all members in all sanghams, planned in the MERIBA Center. It was up to each sangham to decide how much money to spend on the event.

"I don't think we should spend any money on this," one young man said. "Why not give the money to the village?" But another man said, "No, no. Actually, this gathering of the con-gregations is a great highlight and encouragement for us poor people. The exploiters want us to stop. If we do not have this organized event, they will think they have succeeded." Then a third man, poor and illiterate, stood to speak. "Both thoughts are right," he said. "So let's meet only for one day instead of three days. Then the money we would have spent on the other two days can be given to the village." They agreed on this wise idea.

At the day-long meeting of the sanghams, Vijayam was asked to speak to the assembled group. But as he made his way to the front, an old woman stood and started forward. Raising her voice, she called out, "Dr. Vijayam! I want to talk to you." When people tried to stop the woman, Vijayam said, "No, please, I want her to come."

On the platform the old woman said, "I heard that one village lost everything. In our village women work in the fields, and we have saved some money. I want you to take this money to that other village." Then she opened her hand and reached out a dirty piece of cloth with some small coins tied inside it.

For a moment Vijayam was too surprised to speak. But then he said to the woman, "I am not worthy to take your money. You give the gift." Then he asked the women from the other village to come forward so that the old lady could give the coins to them.

The women made their way to the front where they tearfully received the gift. Then the old woman raised her hands and started to sing. It was a beautiful song, one Vijayam immediately recognized. His own father, Bunyan Joseph, had written it. Altogether, the congregation joined in and sang the chorus with her: "It is more cheerful to give than to receive." One by one people put their own offerings on the table. Even Hindu officers stationed at the back of the room offered their contributions.

The poor women who had so carefully saved their money gave about ninety-two rupees to their sisters in need. But the offering they inspired that day came to over one thousand rupees—more than ten times the original gift!

ॐ

"If the Son makes you free, you shall be free indeed."
—John 8:36

CHAPTER 7
FULL-TIME FOR
CHRIST

I n 1987, while Vijayam was still a professor at the university, the vice president of Haggai Institute of Advanced Leadership approached him. He had heard about Vijayam's background and experience in lecturing on the subject of creation versus evolution. "Come to our ten-day Super Servant Seminar on our Maui campus in Hawaii," the vice president urged. "We would like to have you present a talk on the subject of communicating the gospel to the scientific and secular mind."

What an opportunity! Vijayam enthusiastically accepted. While he was there, he presented his ideas not only to the Haggai Institute board members but also to other Christian leaders involved in apologetics. So impressed was President John Haggai with what he heard that at the end of the seminar he invited Vijayam to be a member of the institute's visiting faculty. In this capacity Vijayam could teach in Haggai Institute seminars held at their training centers in Maui and Singapore. So for the next twelve years, Vijayam led seminars in the two locations (in Singapore, he was one of seventy leaders from various theological and professional backgrounds). Attendees were greatly blessed by what they heard, but even more, they were able to put their newfound knowledge to work in their own Christian witness.

Through his association with the alumni trained in Hawaii, Vijayam had the privilege of giving lectures at national seminars throughout India. In preparing for those, he worked with Ravi Zacharias and his international ministry (RZIM) and Hugh Ross, an astrophysicist and president of Reasons to Believe.

After serving as professor and researcher at Osmania University in Hyderabad for thirty years, Vijayam felt an ever-greater burden to serve the Lord full time. With the encouragement of his wife and his father—and in answer to their many prayers—he decided in 1988 to voluntarily retire from the university. He would then be readily available for whatever work the Lord might have for him, particularly in his area of interest—helping and enabling Christian missions. This was an enormous step to take. He was leaving an excellent job to travel down a path that was not at all clear. So he and his wife spent a great deal of time waiting on the Lord in prayer.

At that time Vijayam was also serving as the chairman of Partners International (India), then called Christian Nationals Evangelism Commission (CNEC). Reverend Luis Bush, president of Partners International at the time, went to Hyderabad to attend the Partners International (India) general body meeting. One day while leading the morning devotion, Vijayam shared, "My wife and I are waiting on the Lord to lead us into full-time ministry." As soon as the session was over, Luis Bush approached him with a suggestion: Consider becoming Partners International's regional coordinator for South Asia.

"Give Mary and me six months to pray about it," Vijayam answered. "Then I will give you my decision." Vijayam had no experience in missions. Neither did he have any theological training. Yet, trusting the Lord to provide what he needed, he accepted the position. After all, being regional coordinator would provide wonderful opportunities for him to enable indigenous mission organizations to fulfill their goals. In what other place could he accomplish so much? The leaders of Partners International encouraged him through their constant guidance, through the advice offered at staff meetings, and through training at their headquarters in San Jose, California. (The headquarters has since relocated to Spokane, Washington.)

It had long been Vijayam's dream to study at a seminary. So, in 1992, through the help of Partners International, both Mary and Vijayam attended Dallas Theological Seminary in Dallas, Texas, for a semester. Their course of study included World Missions, Local Church and Evangelism, Spiritual Life, and Science and Theology. In the years since, those studies have proven most helpful to both Mary and Vijayam as the two have systematically made a study of missions, making their involvement with mission organizations even more challenging and meaningful.

The work with Partners International took Vijayam to many parts of India as well as to Bangladesh and Nepal. As he traveled, the Lord gave him opportunities to learn more about the subcontinent—its complex culture, its many and diverse languages and people groups, and its particular world views.

Only God knew how that exposure would affect the future.

❧

"Trust in the Lord with all thine heart;
and lean not unto thine own understanding.
In all thy ways acknowledge him,
and he shall direct thy paths."
—Proverbs 3:5–6, KJV

CHAPTER 8
INDIA FOR
THE KINGDOM
OF GOD

I t was September 30, 1993, the great high day of the ten-day Hindu festival of Ganesh. To ensure good fortune, followers lifted idols of the elephant-headed god of wisdom and prosperity from their places of honor and bore them through the streets. Throngs paraded as the idols were carried into "holy waters," deeper and deeper until the painted forms were completely immersed. That night, to the endless popping of firecrackers, the Vijayams fell into a restless sleep only to be suddenly rattled awake at 4 A.M. The next morning they learned the reason for the early morning disturbance—a devastating earthquake had hit Latur district, in the neighboring state of Maharashtra. In less than one minute, thirty thousand people died.

"Latur district?" Vijayam exclaimed in amazement. As a geologist, he knew that area was the least prone to earthquakes. Of all places, why there?

Vijayam was still pondering that question the next day, when, on a flight to the United States, Jesus' words in Matthew 24:7–8 ran through his mind. When Jesus' disciples ask for signs that the end of the age was drawing near, Jesus answers: "There will be famines and earthquakes in various places. All these are the beginning of birth pains." Famines and earthquakes . . . Just six years earlier, Latur district and the neighboring areas were stricken by a famine that had driven many people to turn to the idol Ganesh, seeking his favor. They were desperate for a new beginning, frantic for good fortune. Vijayam took out his Bible and read on in Matthew 24. It was verse 14 that really gripped his heart: "And this gospel of the kingdom will be preached in the whole world as a testimony to all nations, and then the end will come."

Over the next few months, eighteen more earthquakes occurred in geologically unexpected places throughout the world. All in all, an increasing number of earthquakes have occurred in recent decades, and they have been of ever greater intensity.

On the Ganesh high day of the following year, bubonic plague broke out just north of Latur and quickly engulfed the city of Surat. "There will be great earthquakes, famines and pestilences in various places" (Luke 21:11). These occurrences will be clear warnings of the end of the age. Still, according to Matthew 24, the end will not come until the kingdom is preached *in all the world*. People from *every nation* and *every tongue* must first have a chance to hear the gospel. And of the world's 11,900 people groups, 4,635 are in India. Based on race, culture, and language,

40 percent of the world's "nations" are in that one country alone. So, who will reach all those groups?

Already, under Vijayam's umbrella ministries, much was being done for India. The poor were being empowered and unified under MERIBA. Through the efforts of PROGRESS, training in technologies was helping the poor to help themselves and, despite their caste, to move toward equality. Both MERIBA and PROGRESS were vitally important social movements, and both were meeting great success.

"It is a very good thing to help the village people," Bunyan Joseph said when he saw all that his son was accomplishing. "But what are you doing for evangelism?"

India, the cradle of so many religions, is probably the most religious country in the world. In every area of life, spirituality is a constant presence. Little wonder that many who hear about Jesus Christ ask, "Why do we need any more gods?"

"In India, pure evangelism does not work," says Bishop L. V. Azariah, who was a member of the TENT governing body (see below). "You preach and preach and preach for so many years and see nothing. There are already lots of gurus here. So the other side is important: Why is [Vijayam] doing this? He is doing it in God's name."

Bishop Azariah illustrated with this story: "When I was a seminary student, I was in Bangalore. One night I met a man walking alone on the road. It was pitch dark. I asked him where he was going, and he said he had to work in the morning, but he would spend the night on the road. So my friend and I invited him to spend the night with us. We took him to our room, and I gave him my bed and my pillow. At five in the morning, I stoked the stove to make coffee for him, and then I took him to the train and bought him a ticket. It was there that I first told him I was a Christian. He replied that he was a Muslim. As the train started, I said, 'Goodbye!' He called back, 'Now I know that Jesus Christ is love.'"

Faith and works. Evangelism and social impact—they do indeed go hand in hand.

All his life, Vijayam's father was a "tentmaker"—one who, like the apostle Paul, had a trade that enabled him to support himself as he preached the gospel. And even though Vijayam had always worked in a secular job, tentmaking was an important ministry model for him as well. In a poor country like India, he knew it was vital that those in the ministry be self-supporting. It allows more evangelists to serve among the poor as well as self-sufficient pastors to teach others by example. Little wonder, then, that when he made plans for a school for evangelists and church workers, tentmaking was an important emphasis.

What could be a better name for such an organization than TENT? An acronym for Training for Evangelism, Needs, and Technology, TENT is a place where young men learn about available resources, how to use them, and how to put them to work generating an income for themselves and for fellow workers in their village. It prepares them to support themselves while they preach.

Actual TENT training began in 1986 at Mary and Vijayam's home. The entire class of twenty-five men slept in the hallway. Every morning at 4 A.M. Mary was up cooking for them and preparing for the day. Classes were held all over the house, including on the verandah and in Prakash Nilayam's garage next door. Trainees were unable to pay for the training and their food. They were all too poor. These were humble beginnings for what was to become an amazing ministry.

As trainee classes grew, the Vijayams and Hanumantha Rao located a seven-acre piece of land behind Kondapur village, near Ghatkesar, R. R. District. The land was affordable, but it was also barren and rocky, with poor soil. It did, however, have one promising feature: a hillock that resembled Mount Carmel, the place where the prophet Elijah so effectively and miraculously proclaimed the living God. What setting could be more suitable for training pastors, missionaries, and evangelists?

Actually, the scientists had originally decided on a different piece of land that had more underground water. But one of the clerks superimposed the hydrological map of the first piece onto the geographical map of the second plot. So the second piece of land was bought under the mistaken impression that it had an adequate water supply. Only after the purchase was the mistake discovered. "It was all God's will," Vijayam said in retrospect. "He wanted us to demonstrate what can be done with semiarid land of this kind. After all, the greater part of India is semiarid."

The Water Development Society (WDS), a Christian charitable organization, agreed to dig a bore well for TENT—free of charge. Early in the morning, on the day the well was to be dug, Vijayam prayed earnestly for water. God directed him to Isaiah 35:6: "Water will gush forth in the wilderness and streams in the desert."

A hydrogeological survey had predicted water at a depth of 185 feet. When the digging reached about 160 feet, some moisture should have appeared. But it was only hard granite. The experienced drillers recommended that the drilling be stopped. Drilling farther down, they insisted, was a waste of time and money. TENT staff members hurried to the nearest village to ask Vijayam for guidance. In faith, Vijayam answered, "Go on digging."

At 170 feet there were still no signs of a water-bearing stratum. And none at 180 feet. For the diggers, enough was enough. The sun was blistering hot, and this was obviously wasting valuable time. Ignoring the TENT staff members' pleas, they began packing their equipment. Then Rajan, a TENT employee, jumped onto the digging rig and refused to let it move.

"You are abusing WDS's charitable gift!" the well diggers scolded. But when Rajan steadfastly refused to move, they had no choice but to dig again. At a depth of 186 feet, an explosion shattered the frustrated silence. Water gushed out of the cleft rock, just as it had long ago in the wilderness of Sinai.

More than twenty years later that well continues to supply the major part of TENT's water needs. In fact, it is one of the better wells in the entire village. And it continues to stand as a wonderful testimony to the faithfulness of God.

Today, the land, appropriately named Carmel, is truly magnificent—carpeted with grasses, flowering with everything from marigolds to orchids, and budding biblical-like olives, figs, pomegranates, and grapevines. The farm's mangoes, guavas, and sapotas are like none other. Grafted and trained to just the right height and rate of production, they are the scientific delight of women searching for a microenterprise for themselves, their families, and their villages. Young men (and now women, too) are trained in Carmel's many models and demonstration areas, which include model farms with a vast array of horticultural and floricultural specimens, medicinal plants, ecology displays, a plant nursery, a shade house, a poultry farm, a fish pond, dairy areas, a windmill, a blue-green algae display, and vermin-culture displays. A mechanical workshop for carpentry, a metal shop, areas for work in electronics, and even a kennel are also on the property.

Beautiful though it may be, landscaping is not the purpose. The purpose is for people to learn from the models and then multiply their new skills by passing their knowledge along to others in their village. By this means, men and women are able to bring a means of income into their family. With proper training, even the poorest person can duplicate the enterprise opportunities on display, and each requires very little financial input.

The Carmel campus, however, is far more than just displays. It encompasses sleeping and eating accommodations, classrooms, an auditorium, a beautiful chapel, and a small hostel with a playground. It also includes another 3.75 acres earmarked for the new Bishop Bunyan Joseph Grammar and Technology School.

This program will have a public school curriculum into which local students will be admitted. It will also include a residential school for children of national missionaries and others who desire a good Christian education and vocational training, all with a view to prepare children for future ministry as tentmakers in India.

In addition to technology training, TENT trainees learn methods of both evangelism and ministry to the poor, how to address Christian social concerns, and how to study the Bible. Training is expanding into areas of counseling and working with families as well as music and drama.

One indispensable instructor is P. T. George. "Professor George has been my best friend for many years," said Vijayam. "God has given him extraordinary intelligence and the gift of interpreting the Word of God, which he does with much eagerness. Whenever I need some explanation, clarification, or commentary on a passage from the Scriptures, I seek his help. He has also helped me in writing papers and articles that I have presented in seminars, retreats, and training programs. He encouraged me to start TENT ministry and donated the seed money for several projects within that ministry. And he gives training to evangelists during TENT workshops. Not only was he the first chairman of the board but he has also accompanied me on some of my visits to partner ministries in India and Bangladesh."

Two of the Vijayams' sons-in-law have also been involved in PROGRESS and TENT: Milton, husband of their eldest daughter Mary Lois Vyjayanthi, and Uday Kumar, husband of second daughter Rhoda Vidya Sravanthi. Youngest daughter Ruth

Prakashmani Lajwanthi and her engineer husband Rajshekar are extremely supportive of the ministry. Son Joseph Vijaywanth, with the prayerful encouragement of his wife Suneetha, will succeed his father in overseeing the ministries.

And now—after the famines, after the plagues, after the Latur earthquake—the question: Who will take the gospel of Jesus Christ to the peoples of India? Not just the usual targeted peoples, but *all* the peoples? And when?

Until recently missionaries concentrated on preaching to society's outcasts and to nominal Christians—people known to be relatively open to the gospel. Mostly they have stayed away from the hard-to-reach Hindus and Muslims. Yet Hindus and Muslims make up more than 90 percent of India's population. That is why, despite the fact that parts of India have some of the highest concentrations of Christians in the world, the country still has more unreached people groups than any other major region on earth—over 4,000 groups. Also, a full 85 percent of the 1,386 tribal and outcast groups are still unreached. Even more, most of these are not just unreached, they are not even considered.

To reach them all, Vijayam figured "it would take a force of 40,000 witnesses, an average of ten for each of the 4,000 unreached people groups in India." He considered it an impossible task—it simply could not be done. And yet, Vijayam could not get the idea out of his mind.

Two years later, in 1995, Vijayam shared his vision with Partners International. He explained to them that a number of agencies were already researching India's widely scattered people groups, but the information needed to be organized and mapped. Then forty thousand church planters must be trained— able, committed trainees drawn from among the various people groups. They didn't have to be educated, but they must have a burden to witness and should be selected with the assistance of missions and churches. They would be trained in church planting and church growth as well as in cultural issues and communication skills. And they must have productive trades. Since nothing could be accomplished for the Lord without prayer, the first order that Vijayam proposed was to mobilize a prayer force of eighty thousand people—two for each worker and the worker's people group.

And so Joshua Vision India (JVI) was born. Simply put, JVI is a vision and strategy for reaching each of India's unreached groups. Its object is to train and deploy a harvest force of forty thousand grassroots workers to get the job done. Of course, JVI cannot train all these people directly, so each year the organization trains Master Trainers. Each Master Trainer does field research and becomes well acquainted with a specific unreached people group to then prepare a strategy suited for that chosen people group. The Master Trainers train groups of grassroots workers and, with the workers' help, implement the prepared strategy. From the variety of cutting-edge tentmaking possibilities provided them by PROGRESS scientists, both Master Trainers and Harvesters learn appropriate technologies to support and sustain them in the field. Scientist Rama Rao said, "We train Master Trainers and Harvesters at the farm. We teach them in the class, and then we take them to the field."

As men were trained, committed women who also had leadership potential began to ask, "Why not us also?"

Half of India's billion-plus population is made up of women, more than 80 percent of them living in rural areas. Seventy percent of Indian families live below the poverty level of less than $350 (U.S.) per year. More than half the women are illiterate and live in ignorance and oppression—often oppressed by their own family. Because baby girls are undervalued, in hard economic situations they are underfed or starved, sometimes even killed. Girls are kept at home to work instead of being sent to school. And the dowry system gravely deepens the plight of women. Economically dependent, often intimidated and exploited by drinking or violent men, women do far more work than men. According to the World Health Organization, rural Indian women are the hardest-working people in the world.

Yet Indian women are the mothers of the family, the ones who nurture, care for, and provide the greatest education for India's next generation. Women's great potential is clear from the success of the sanghams, where women develop the habit of saving money. Many get microloans at low interest rates to fund small enterprises such as raising animals, growing crops, or even running shops. Encouraged by the 100 percent repayment of these loans, the United Nations Development Program and other development agencies assist the program with grants. Now women can get loans for as much as five thousand rupees. And because they have learned to save, many women are now able to pay their children's school fees, even at the college level. They can meet medical expenses and build better houses, too. They even help the church financially.

It is also true that women can take the gospel where men are not culturally welcome—to other women. And so in 2001, the Lord gave Mary Vijayam the burden to start a training program for women. IWILL (Indian Women in Lord's Labor) provides shorter, specialized training courses specifically designed for women leaders. For six months, women Master Trainers are schooled in holistic evangelism. Then they train grassroots women Harvesters. IWILL focuses on women's problems and needs and on empowering women through self-help groups.

Amazingly, this women's movement has grown more rapidly than the men's. Overall, women have surpassed the men in commitment to evangelism and effectiveness in the area of contextual technology.

The message of the gospel is doubly good news for Indian women, because it provides not only eternal salvation but also a new status and significance for the downtrodden in this life. And women are by far the best ones to reach other women with the gospel of Jesus Christ and his love and liberation. Even as quiet teachers and custodians of religion in their own home, women who know Christ can bring entire families—and even entire villages—to a saving knowledge of Christ. "These women have brought new hope to our village," one grateful woman in a tsunami-hit village said of the women Harvesters sent by the Church Growth Research Association (CGRA) for IWILL training. Women can also mobilize other women to pray. But with such a wide-open field for women Harvesters, the great need is for Master Trainers to train them.

Why would God choose a scientist—a university professor—to bring the gospel to all the peoples and tribes of India? Why not a seminary-trained pastor? Or a full-time missionary? Better yet, why not a world-renowned preacher?

Could it be because Vijayam made himself available to God? That he was more interested in the plight of the poor and suffering than in providing himself a comfortable life? That when he saw injustice in the world, he asked, "Lord, what would you have me to do?"

Imagine what would happen if every child of God fell before the Lord with that same question: "Lord, what would you have *me* to do?"

Imagine!

&

"Because of the LORD's great love we are not consumed,
for his compassions never fail.
They are new every morning; great is your faithfulness."
—Lamentations 3:22–23

CHAPTER 9
THE POWER OF ONE
MULTIPLIED

In India many young Christians, in answer to God's call, are training at JVI and IWILL as Master Trainers. It is their desire to be fully equipped as they help to carry the good news of Jesus Christ to unreached people groups across their country. And, as Jesus did in his own ministry, they want to be able to meet people's desperate physical and emotional needs as well as their spiritual needs. Armed with both Bible training and top-rate technologies, some Christians are even venturing across India's borders into forbidding areas where few Westerners dare to go, let alone attempt to preach the gospel.

Come and meet this new generation of Indian missionaries.

Jaspina
Touching Children in Tamil Nadu

Dressed in a striking sari splashed with shimmering gold, Jaspina looked regal. That she hailed from the privileged Brahmin caste was not the least bit surprising. Everything in her appearance, her actions, her speech, and her demeanor spoke of high breeding. Jaspina's mother is a Christian, her father a Hindu. But both mother and father love their daughter dearly, and both were mystified and distressed when Jaspina chose to spend her life among a desperately poor tribal group in the southern Indian state of Tamil Nadu.

"Not one person in that tribal area can read or write," Jaspina said in a soft, urgent voice. "The children do not even know their letters. So I am teaching them to read."

Of course, life in the tribal village is nothing like the life to which Jaspina was accustomed. She acknowledged as much with a self-conscious laugh. "But I do not need comfort to be happy," she quickly added. And what of her gold sari? "I do not wear it in the village," Jaspina said. "There I wear what the villagers wear."

When she first arrived in the tribal village, however, she brought her nice saris with her. On that first day, when she walked out to the village, well-bedecked in silk and beads and sequins, the village women gathered around to gasp and stare. A little girl ventured forward and reached toward Jaspina's beautiful clothes, but her mother snatched her back, issuing a sharp warning loud enough for all the children to hear: Never touch the fine lady! The village women would not allow Jaspina to drink from the community cup that hung on the side of the well. It was not good enough for such a one as she, they insisted. When Jaspina protested and attempted to reach out to them, the women bowed on the ground and worshiped her.

"I never wore those saris again," Jaspina said. "This that I wear today is my wedding sari. I will wear it here, but when I go back to the village, I will leave it in my mother's wardrobe."

Jaspina and her new husband allowed themselves two weeks with their families before heading together to the tribal village. "My husband will start a church there," Jaspina said, flashing her shy smile. "We want to serve the Lord together."

Bharat
Reaching into Nepal through West Bengal

Both Bharat and his wife grew up in well-to-do Nepalese families. Both families were Hindu, yet both allowed their children to go to Christian Sunday school. And although their families were strongly opposed to it, both Bharat and his wife made an independent decision to be a follower of Jesus Christ. "There are many tribes among the Nepalese," Bharat said. "And very, very few of our people are Christians."

Although he is from a high caste family and is well spoken and highly educated, Bharat is not at all popular in his home area of Darjeeling. That is because he preaches Christianity, something the local Brahmans insist he has no right to do. Neither do they like that he mixes so freely with low caste people. "I face much persecution," he said. "The Brahmans throw stones at me, especially now that a few people are showing an interest in what I have to say." And now that Bharat's wife is expecting their first child, the Brahmans have let the couple know that children of Christians are not welcome in the local schools.

Still, Bharat said that the people in his area are very hungry for God. They show it by desperately reaching out for any god. "Already the Hindus have so many gods, yet if they see something as ordinary as a different kind of stone, they exclaim, 'Oh, this must be a god!' and they worship it, too."

Unfortunately, not many people are prepared to tell the people about the true God. "The few Christians who are there are not much qualified or biblically grounded," Bharat explained. "They are too afraid to preach the gospel. Many just hand out tracts, then they stand back and hope people will come and ask them about Jesus."

This is why Bharat and his wife are committed to educating, training, and equipping leaders in their area of eastern India. "Train up leaders," Bharat insisted. "Then just see what God will do!"

Amit
Reaching Out to Tribal People in Orissa

Black magic. Evil powers. Witchcraft. People use these words when they talk about the Indian state of Orissa. And it's all true, according to Amit. Sickness comes through evil powers, he explained, because people serve the evil spirits and practice witchcraft. Little surprise, then, that the people of Orissa are especially resistant to the gospel. "It is a very hard place to be a Christian," Amit said. "Especially for those who go out into the tribal areas. Most people in Orissa are unreached."

Amit should know. He himself comes from a place of black magic. "The people in my area are blind," he said, shaking his head sadly. "They are like a frog in the well that cannot get out alone. I want to open their eyes to what the gospel says. I want them to know that their sins can be forgiven."

Yet fear and danger are huge hurdles in this forbidding area where an anticonversion law makes it illegal to, in any way, influence another person to change religions. "Where I live, the church was bombed, and the houses of all the Christians were burned," Amit recalled. "The Christians all ran to the mountains to hide. It is very difficult to give the gospel to people who live in terror."

When Amit hands out tracts, his face is slapped. When he dares to speak of Jesus, death threats are yelled to him. "The people are so poor. Many are hungry. In entire villages not one person can read or write," Amit said. "If we can go to them with technologies, we can show them how they can earn money so they can support their families. It is a way to help their lives with social development and to earn the right to show them spiritual answers. We must give them the gospel, but we also have a responsibility to meet their great physical needs."

Priyani
Counseling Services for Women in Orissa

In the harsh state of Orissa, twenty-two-year-old Priyani ministers to the married women of the area who struggle alone against so many difficulties. In an innovative program, she uses Bible stories as a springboard for counseling them. Never before have these women had the luxury of a caring person who was eager to listen to them and able to offer them guidance. "So many problem situations they are facing," Priyani said with a sigh. "And they have nothing or no one to help them or guide them."

Priyani's eyes filled with tears as she told of a young wife who set herself on fire and burned to death in front of her house as her little ones looked on in horror. "She did it because her life was hopeless," Priyani said. "Her family paid her husband the required dowry for marriage, but then he started to demand more and more money from them. He said if they didn't pay, he would get a divorce and his wife would be left to beg on the streets with the children. So her family paid as long as they could manage it. But when they could not pay any more, he divorced her and threw her out of his parents' house."

This meant she had no place to live. No where to go. No food for her children. And no way to earn a living. "She could not bear such a life," Priyani said, "so she chose to die." Then, after a pause: "If she could have talked to someone about options, maybe it would have been different." This is why Priyani is ministering in Orissa.

She also told of a woman who took a chicken, lifted it high, and entreated a spirit to help her torture her son's wife. "Whatever she did to the chicken would happen to her daughter-in-law," Priyani said. "She would not kill the chicken, just torture it. I watched the girl get worse and worse. When the woman broke the chicken's leg, her daughter-in-law fell down screaming in pain, and she couldn't walk."

Priyani called the Christians together to pray. Some were too frightened to join in, but Priyani led the others in a prayer vigil. "I understood those who didn't join us, because I was scared, too. I knew it was dangerous for us," Priyani said. "But when the chicken died and the girl was set free, it proved to the people that it was God who has the real power."

This is why Priyani is ministering in Orissa.

Nilesh
Hope for Tribal People of Maharastra

When Nilesh decided to go to the unreached tribal areas in the arid lands of the state of Maharastra, he was well aware of what he was getting into. He knew few Christians live there. He knew the population was largely Muslim, and he knew poverty was rampant and crushing. "In Maharastra I can talk about Christ in my home, but I cannot stand in the street and preach in public," Nilesh said. "Anyone who does that will immediately be arrested."

Nilesh began his work as a pastor of a house church in the area where he grew up. But although the people around him desperately needed to know Jesus as Savior, his heart ached to reach the many unreached tribal groups scattered beyond his hometown. That's where he longed to go. "It does not make sense to go to them," his friends cautioned. "Tribal people speak languages you do not know. Their cultures are not your culture. You do not understand their rituals. Here, where you belong, you have trouble because you are a Christian. Out there, where you do not even belong, they will kill you."

Nilesh knew that everything they said was true. And yet he went. In fact, he visited every home in each tribal area around his village—every one. And, surprisingly, everywhere he went he was welcomed.

Why?

"God has given me talents of singing and writing songs," Nilesh said. "I can communicate through music even when I don't know the language or the ways of the people. So I decided to take my songs and go ahead into the tribal areas and trust God to make the way for me."

And make a way God did. Today Nilesh focuses on tribal families. He begins by introducing education. The people are not only unable to read, they have never even seen a book. Just to hold one in their hands is a wondrous thing. "But I do not want to only teach them to read and write," he said. "I want to teach them to *think* as well, to *reason*, and to *understand*. The Bible is a wonderful place to begin."

Nilesh is committed to educating tribal people in Maharastra, but his commitment does not stop there. He is also guiding them to know and understand their legal rights. And he is leading them in an intensive study of the Bible. One by one, those who had previously never heard the name of Jesus are claiming him as their own personal Savior.

"God gave me vision to reach the people of my state despite what might happen to me," Nilesh said. "Whatever it is, I will be faithful to God."

Pradip
Tribes Reaching Out to Others in Assam

Conflicting loyalties, simmering within the people living in the far northeastern state of Assam, should come as no surprise to anyone with knowledge of the area. The long fingers of the state of Assam closely border China to the north, Myanmar (Burma) to the west, and Bangladesh to the south. And many of the tribal peoples in the area are determined to see Assam become a separate state. Pradip is sympathetic to the passions of the people. He is, after all, one of them. He belongs to the Boro tribe.

Interestingly, the tribal people in Assam are the Christians. Living among animists and Muslims and Hindus, tribal Christians carry the gospel outside their tribal areas to the unreached people around them.

"They say to me, 'We are higher caste than you are. So why should we listen to you low caste people?'" Pradip said of his caste-conscious Hindu Indian neighbors. "But they are wrong. There is no caste among the tribes. We are all one."

The answer to reaching these people, Pradip believes, is through children. He said, "Many people are so poor that they are not able to care for their children. So they abandon them on the street. That's why I have started a children's care home."

Pradip understands an exceedingly important principle: "By reaching the children, it is possible to change the next generation." And his three-way hope for the next generation is lofty indeed: to make education available to the children, to offer a way out of the area's crushing poverty, and to point the people to spiritual hope through Jesus Christ.

"Right now, their only hope is to make their own state, because they think that will make everything different," Pradip said. "But right now, if they had their own state, they would only carry the same problems over with them. Something must change both their physical poverty and their spiritual poverty." To that end, Pradip is in the process of raising holistically trained spiritual leaders. "I want to be a good leader for the people of God," he said.

He has started well, for already there are about 120 people in his local church. And on their behalf, Pradip asked this prayer request: "Please pray that we should all be faithful people of God."

Asong
To Burma via Manipur

Not too many years ago, Asong's grandparents were animists who worshiped the sun and moon, the trees and rocks. Then the tribal ruler at the time heard about Jesus Christ, and he became a follower, a Christian. So the entire tribal community followed his lead, also accepting Christ. That's the way things were done back then.

"My community is Christian," Asong reported, "but most are not committed. In fact, it is hard to find a committed Christian there. It is a big problem."

Nestled against Burma, in the state of Manipur, there are still those who speak of insurgency. "Many of them are from a

Christian background," Asong said. "The ground problem that stirs such talk is poverty. And that we don't look like Indians. They say we are not from India really. They say that Burma is my heritage. From my home, it only takes about an hour to get to Burma. Just a fifteen-rupee bus ride. That's how close I am to people who are like me but have never heard the gospel."

Asong feels certain that God wants him to call the church in his homeland of Manipur to revival. "The church is there, but only on Sundays," he says. "After that, everyone goes back to the old way of life for the rest of the week. More and more, we are a copy of the church in the West."

Other men and women from Manipur are also working to awaken the sleeping church. They, too, are training new leaders. And like Asong, they are carrying the gospel of Jesus Christ across the forbidden border into Burma.

Haopu
Taking the Gospel into Bhutan

"I am taking the gospel of Jesus Christ into Bhutan," Haopu said with a surprisingly casual air. Bhutan? The country thought to have fewer than three thousand Christians? Where not one missionary is believed to be operating? Bhutan, where even house church services must be conducted in secrecy? Why Bhutan?

"Why not Bhutan?" Haopu asked. "It is one of the least evangelized countries in the world. People there badly need the gospel. Where would be a better place for me to serve Christ?" Haopu is an intelligent, well-educated young man. He has a master of divinity degree. But what possible good will that do him in Bhutan? He certainly will not be allowed to preach!

"That's why I went to JVI for training," Haopu explained. "I wanted to learn all about technologies and how they can be used to help the poor. I wanted to learn practical applications for a holistic approach to ministry."

"I am willing to work as a laborer," Haopu said. In fact, that is precisely what he expects to do. Whatever it takes, he will do it. And one other Master Trainer is already at work in the country, quietly applying a holistic approach. So a small work has already been started.

Haopu is actually from the state of Manipur. But while many from Manipur have gone across the border into Burma, few have ventured into the more forbidding country of Bhutan, which is why Haopu feels so strongly about going there.

"They need to know, too," Haopu said, his voice edged in urgency. "If those early British Christians had stayed away from Nagaland and Manipur two hundred years ago because it was too difficult and they were too afraid, we would not be here today. Now it is our turn. Now we must do whatever we can do to tell others."

Moala
Isolated Tribes in Arunachal Pradesh

Nagaland is the most Christian state in India. A full 90 percent of its population claim to be Christian. Nagaland also boasts an exceptionally high literacy rate. And people there are not plagued by societal challenges such as the caste system, abuse of women, and crushing dowry demands. Certainly, a great deal of work remains to be done in Nagaland. But as one would expect, many young people from this state on India's far northeastern border with Burma eagerly come to participate in Vijayam's vision to reach the unreached of India. A disproportionately large number of people, both men and women, come to JVI and IWILL from Nagaland. People such as Moala, whose high cheekbones and marked Asian features belie her tribal ancestry.

"Our ancestors were headhunters who worshiped the sun and gods of stone," Moala said. "But when British Christians came to Nagaland two hundred years ago, our people responded to their message. The Christians established churches, schools, and Bible colleges. We are very much indebted to those missionaries."

Perhaps that explains why Moala made the ministry decisions she has made. She left the comfort and prosperity of Nagaland and went farther north to the state of Arunachal Pradesh, which lies high in the Himalayas and shares a border with Tibet. It is not friendly country. Even then, Moala hiked far into the isolated countryside to find the villages of the people she especially wanted to know—tribal people that time seemed to have forgotten. Worshipers of the sun and moon, their lives had not changed for centuries. They had no knowledge of telephones, or televisions, or houses that were anything other than one-room shelters, or any form of transportation except their own feet. They knew nothing of sanitation, basic health care, adequate nutrition, and medicine. Of course, they could not read or write. They didn't even have a written language. Grinding poverty and the ever present fear that at any moment angry gods might rain down disaster on them drove their lives.

Moala hiked in and settled among the villagers, and she gave them hope. From her backpack, Moala pulled out clothes for the shivering children. She worked in the fields alongside the women. She taught mothers to wash their hands before using them to prepare food so their little ones would not be so quick to get sick or die. She showed the women her Bible, and she began to teach them to read words. She learned the people's language. She sang them songs and told stories about Jesus, and she prayed with them. And the women welcomed her and rejoiced that they could also be followers of Christ.

In November of 2005, the Vijayams held a huge gathering, inviting all the Master Trainers who could manage to come back to JVI in Hyderabad for a weekend of instruction, renewal, sharing, and encouragement. Moala went, taking with her twelve wide-eyed tribeswomen. In six arduous days, the women accomplished something they never dreamed possible: they walked, rode a train, traveled by bus and finally by taxi all the way from the Himalayan foothills to southern India—a terrifyingly wondrous experience for women who had never been farther from their house than the fields in which they toiled from dawn to dusk.

Because they were just learning to read and write, Mary Vijayam crafted a course specifically designed for nonliterate beginners hungry for God's Word. Moala acted as translator. At the end of the gathering, each of the twelve women proudly walked across the platform to receive a certificate of completion. "Living in our village is like living in darkness," one tribeswoman said. "Now for the first time I see the light."

That is the goal of every Master Trainer: to take the Light of the World to places that know only darkness.

What would happen if it were the goal of every follower of Christ, in every country, all around the world?

~

"After this I looked and there before me was
a great multitude that no one could count,
from every nation, tribe, people and language,
standing before the throne and in front of the Lamb.
They were wearing white robes and were holding palm
branches in their hands. And they cried out in a loud voice:
'Salvation belongs to our God,
who sits on the throne, and to the Lamb.'"
—Revelation 7:9–10

CHAPTER 10
A FAMILY
MATTER

I f anyone recognizes the paradox of India, it is Vijayam. He has famously described his country this way: "India is like a nuclear missile being carried to the launch pad on the back of an oxcart." Concise and right on point, just like Vijayam's approach to each area of his own life. Just like his strategy to spread God's love throughout India.

Indian Christians, North American Christians, African Christians, Asian Christians, believers who live in Europe, in Burma, in Mexico, in Sudan—all are unique. Each comes with specific cultural sensitivities and sensibilities. Each brings insights, and each suffers from blind spots. Each shoulders great strengths, and each is burdened by weaknesses. This is precisely why each of us needs the others.

All around the world, those who confess Jesus Christ as Lord and Savior are part of one great family. All are brothers and sisters. All will spend eternity together. But we need not look long or hard to see that great disparities exist between places, and people, and circumstances. Huge inequities exist between countries and within countries: the rich and prosperous versus those barely scraping by at poverty level; the highly educated versus the illiterate; nuclear missiles versus oxcarts.

Numbing poverty, injustice, and oppression are sad facts of life in far too many areas of the world. And to our shame, many who claim the name of Christ are perfectly content to stay comfortable. Consciously or not, too many choose to distance themselves from those who suffer.

From one end of the earth to the other, we who claim the name of Christ are family. And the truth is that our Father God has no favorites among us. He makes his impartiality perfectly clear in his Word, from the beginning of the nation of Israel (Deuteronomy 10:17). Still, human nature consistently persuades those who find themselves in a position of privilege or power to consider themselves favored by God. And so the biblical lesson must be taught and retaught: "I now realize how true it is that God does not show favoritism but accepts men from every nation who fear him and do what is right" (Acts 10:34–35).

Why, then, are some people so comfortable, with their stomachs round and full and their wallets heavy, while others struggle along in poverty doing their best to keep their children alive? Why does an impartial God, who is no respecter of persons, heap so many gifts on some while he allows others to cry out in want and oppression? And why do some have endless opportunities for salvation while others have never once heard the name of Jesus?

Hard questions to be sure. We live in a world of sin and un-righteousness. That's true for all people everywhere, for Christians and non-Christians alike. Yet it is also true that God has freely given gifts to all his children—talents, resources, opportunities, and salvation. In whatever portion an individual receives them, all are nevertheless gifts from God. And Jesus said, "Freely you have received, freely give" (Matthew 10:8).

So let us refocus the basic question: Be it much or be it little, what are you doing with what God has entrusted to you? The possessions with which each of us is blessed were given for a reason; they are intended for the benefit of all people. Repeatedly Jesus laid out the principle that his followers are not to rejoice in earthly possessions. Neither are they to become attached to them. This is true of finances, and it is true of special gifts and abilities. It is even true of spiritual gifts. Followers of Christ are to rejoice in what they are able to share.

From the beginning, receiving a blessing required *being* a blessing in return. When God called Abraham out of his home-land, God made a covenant with him that he would make of Abraham a great nation (Genesis 12:1–3). That covenant com-bined with a promise—"I will bless you and make your name great"—and a requirement—"You shall be a blessing" (NASB). Not *maybe* you will be a blessing. Not *hopefully* you will find it in your heart to be a blessing. But "You *shall* be a blessing."

Still, some in the family of God have a far more comfortable life than others. They certainly seem to be disproportionately blessed by God. For these, the Holy Spirit led Timothy to write this further admonition: "Command those who are rich in this present world not to be arrogant nor to put their hope in wealth, which is so uncertain, but to put their hope in God, who richly provides us with everything for our enjoyment. Command them to do good, to be rich in good deeds, and to be generous and willing to share. In this way they will lay up treasure for themselves as a firm foundation for the coming age, so that they may take hold of the life that is truly life" (1 Timothy 6:17–19).

"*You shall* be a blessing!"

Vijayam followed these guidelines when he made the decision to live in India and work on behalf of the poor rather than pursue a more luxurious life in the West. Mary Vijayam followed these guidelines when she encouraged her husband to leave the university to go full time into the Lord's work. Also following biblical guidelines are the generous donors whose gifts enable much of the work at JVI to go forward and the partners in various parts of the world who support the Indian workers taking the gospel into unreached areas.

In the 1700s, the Industrial Revolution brought about great changes in agriculture, manufacturing, and transportation, changes that profoundly altered the socioeconomic and cultural conditions in the West. For the first time it was possible for people to actually create wealth. Imagine what might have happened if this wealth had been shared around the world in the spirit of Christ. But because the spirit of Christ is not the reality of nations, stronger nations used their wealth to build their own well-to-do class, and then they armed themselves and marched out to colonize the unindustrialized nations. The rich became extremely wealthy, and the poor sank to new depths of poverty. The powerful rose to be masters, and those without power slid lower and lower until they were slaves.

It was Lenin who finally marched in, proclaiming a solution: Marxist communism. No more haves and have nots, he promised. No more rich and poor. Instead, he would create a utopia for the masses.

And the masses responded. What had the government done for the people, anyway? Nothing! And the church? She stood by and watched in silence. Only the communists held out hope. But human nature does not change. And as young Vijayam discovered, communism's remedy proved to be worse than the disease it promised to cure.

As the British colonized India, they built hospitals for the many English who were falling sick with tropical diseases and schools to teach Indians the English language. Of course, that meant they needed teachers and doctors. But not many English men and women were willing to leave the cool climes of England for the steamy hot, mosquito-infested jungles of India. It was mainly Christians who went. The opportunity to take the Word of God to people who had never heard the name of Jesus compelled them. In time, India gained a grim reputation as the graveyard of missionaries.

But out of an evil time, good came.

When missionaries carried the gospel to Naga headhunters (Moala's ancestors), the message was welcomed and received. Christianity quickly spread throughout the area. Others also received it, including a bright, orphan boy who would take the name of Gideon Bunyan.

But mostly, the missionaries only went to the segments of the population they considered most promising. Only a favored few Indians were educated, and they were the ones who were later placed in positions of power. This produced new, enhanced divisions of haves and have nots—educated versus illiterate, chosen versus rejected.

But that was then. The twenty-first century is a different age entirely.

When Jon Lewis, president of Partners International, speaks of the state of world missions, he points to the book of Acts. In Acts 1–11, all mission activity centered on Jerusalem. It was the focal point of all Christian outreach. Great and wonderful things happened there—miracles, healings, huge numbers of people coming to faith.

Then, with startling suddenness, everything changes in Acts 12. James, the brother of John and one of Jesus' inner circle, is dead, beheaded by King Herod. And that's not all—Peter is in prison and scheduled for trial. It would not be long before he too would die.

In Acts 13 a group of men, gathered from all nations, sets out on a missionary trip. But they do not leave from Jerusalem as one would expect. No, this time they leave from Antioch, a Gentile city. And from that point on, Jerusalem is never again the center of mission sending. Its time had passed.

Yet, change comes hard. People do not easily give up their old, familiar ways. And so, in Acts 15, we witness the clash—the old Jewish way versus the new Gentile way. But a wonderful thing happens in this chapter. A debate takes place, old approach versus new approach. And each side actually stops insisting that it is right long enough to listen to the other side. Together they reach an agreement, a partnership.

"Interesting," you may say, "but what does that have to do with us today?" "Everything," says Jon Lewis. When it comes to the seat of mission activity, he sees a definite parallel between Jerusalem and the West. Despite mistakes and a checkered history, for three hundred years the West has been the sending point for missionaries. And God has blessed those efforts. Many wonderful results have come from the work of those years—schools have been built, hospitals established, and the Bible translated into many languages and taught to countless people and tribes. All this time the West has been living out Acts 1–11.

But on September 11, 2001, al-Qaeda terrorists hijacked passenger airplanes and flew them into the twin towers of the World Trade Center in New York City. That morning, when 2,998 Americans died, everything changed. It was the West's equivalent of Acts 12. Now, Jon Lewis believes, we are living in an Acts 13 world. No longer is the West the center of Christian missionary activity. Now, men and women from all nations must work together in a completely new way. It isn't easy, because it is not the way we are used to operating. But it is imperative that we come together in Acts 15 style and reach an agreement so that we can work together in harmony.

The new paradigm, then, is this:

resources + opportunities = a new partnership

Both East and West can learn lessons from history. Development and progress must be approached from a *holistic* standpoint. That is, it must take into consideration the body, the mind, and the soul of an individual and indeed of an entire society. Spiritual development is foundational. For unless social development has an ethical foundation, sustainability is not possible. Professor George, who works alongside Vijayam, goes so far as to say, "Material development without spiritual and ethical development will ultimately lead to destruction and a curse."

Vijayam's programs, MERIBA and PROGRESS, are excellent examples. Early on, Partners International and other Christian groups, as well as individual Christians, saw the potential and donated financially to what they knew to be investments for the kingdom of God. Now, because of the solid holistic foundations set in the beginning, both MERIBA and PROGRESS are accomplishing their humanitarian goals and have attracted the attention of the government, something that never would have happened had they been more one-sided. This holistic foundation is even true with JVI, since it is the technology that opens the door to the gospel in so many places. (Remember Haopu in Bhutan?)

"Everyone wants my money," an exasperated Western donor said. "I can't give to everyone. I can't fund every project. I simply cannot meet everyone's needs."

No. No one can. So then, "Why does God make so many poor people?" some ask, as did little Vijayam as he bounced over the Indian countryside in the back of his father's bullock cart.

In every one of the four gospels—Matthew, Mark, Luke, and John—we read the account of a woman who broke open a valuable alabaster jar and reverently poured its contents of expensive perfume over Jesus' head. "Such a waste!" his disciples grumbled. "We could have sold that for more than a year's wages and then given the money to the poor!"

Jesus was not the least bit impressed with his disciples' seemingly charitable attitude. Instead, he praised the woman's beautiful deed. "The poor you will always have with you," he said, "but you will not always have me" (Matthew 26:11, NIV). (It is important to note that this one-of-a-kind illustration from Jesus occurred just days before he was crucified. The stunning preparation for burial foretold a particular event—his sacrificial death.)

We too always have the poor with us. The chasm between those who have and those who need is as wide as ever. And it includes sisters and brothers in the family of God. Food and education, medical care and emergency aid, and financial help for global Christian efforts—these needs can be met only when the ones who have the resources share them wisely and prayerfully with those who have the opportunities to most effectively make a difference. But is this happening?

A 15-year study conducted by Empty Tomb, a mission research and advocacy organization in Champaign, Illinois, indicates that in recent years a mere two cents out of each dollar donated in North American Protestant churches goes for overseas mission work. Just two pennies! By far the greatest percentage of church income goes to fund the large church "campuses" that are so popular today and to support the burgeoning staff helping churches with their abundance of internal programs. Is this really what Jesus meant when he praised the woman for doing a "beautiful deed" for him? Does he truly advocate bypassing opportunities in the two-thirds world in order for Western Christians to have more programs and entertainment?

In Acts 20:35, Paul quoted these more pointed words of Jesus: "It is more blessed to give than to receive." They sound amazingly similar to the words God spoke to Abraham, don't they? Both an invitation and an order. Jesus was saying, "You *be* a blessing!" Still today, Jesus is saying the same thing to his followers all around the world.

The greatest enrichment initiatives North American Christians can put into motion in their congregation has nothing to do with internal programs and a large staff. It comes from gratefully acknowledging the blessings poured out on them from God's gracious hand and then asking him to show them a better way. It means that those who have the resources work in partnership with those who have the opportunities so that together they can effect a powerful force for missions in the twenty-first century.

But wait. There's more.

Sharing what we have in this way—resources and opportunities—actually brings honor to God. In fact, God gives special honor to those who dig deep and give to the very limit of their capacity. Standing in the temple, Jesus looked right past the rich men who so enjoyed making a great show of placing their large gifts in the temple treasury and focused instead on one poor widow who quietly dropped two tiny copper coins into the box. In Luke 21:3–4 we read these words from Jesus, "This poor widow has put in more than all the others. All these people gave their gifts out of their wealth; but she out of her poverty put in all she had to live on."

Certainly, poverty, injustice, and oppression in the world should never cease to cause us pain, even to the most wealthy and comfortable among us. Suffering among fellow Christians should be especially agonizing to us, for they are family. But many things are not as they should be. When well-to-do Christians spend great amounts of money on personal luxuries, yet remain unmoved by the plight of the poor and oppressed, it sends a distinct message to the world about the true priorities of those who profess to follow Christ.

Words about personal beliefs mean little when they are not followed by deeds. Lectures about the equality of every man, woman, and child in the eyes of God, not backed by personal action, result in ridicule. For the way Christians choose to handle their personal resources shouts the truth about the state of their heart. This is true in the United States, and Canada, and Australia, and Europe, and it is true in India, Africa, and all around the world.

Bunyan Joseph did not pause to ask how much he was required to give to God. Such a question would never have occurred to him. He simply opened his pockets and gave everything. Sadhu Sundar Singh never asked, either. He willingly walked away from a life of riches and comfort and into a life of obedience. Countless others throughout the ages, including the apostle Paul, have sought to, first and foremost, follow Christ without stopping to count the cost. They understood that they were simply stewards of whatever God put into their hands. Be it more or be it less, it was not theirs. Resources and opportunities, all were entrusted to them by the Master to be used for his purposes. So that is what they did.

With great blessing comes great responsibility. In Luke 12:48 we read that from everyone who has been given much, much will be demanded; and from the one who has been entrusted with much, much more will be asked.

We are the family of God. We are partners in the Lord's work. And we carry within us the answer to world peace. That answer does not come through power, neither does it come through politics. The answer is not seizing control of the earth's natural resources or amassing the greatest hoard of wealth. It has nothing to do with commanding the greatest armies on earth. No, the answer to world peace lies within the Christian message: sharing, atoning, forgiving, reconciling. The way of peace comes through the cross.

"In ancient times, India was the great melting pot of races, cultures, and languages," said Vijayam. "Today, the modern melting pot of the world is the United States of America." In addition, he pointed out, with each year that goes by, the nations of the world are increasingly multicultural and multiethnic.

Professor B. E. Vijayam, Ph.D.—university professor; renowned, award-winning scientist; founder of MERIBA, PROGRESS, TENT, and JVI—made a career of reaching India's poorest people with God's love. And he reminds his Christian brothers and sisters in the United States, as he does in India, that in obedience to the Lord's command, specific and urgent efforts must be made to reach out to every one of the many and divergent people groups. "Those who accept Christ should purposely look for other people groups to reach," he said. "But for this to happen, it is essential that they be equipped with special training."

It just so happens that the curriculum for such a training program is ready and waiting. Already developed by Joshua Vision India, already tried and tested many times over, already supported by the experiences of many who have used it successfully, this curriculum is ready to be shared with any church or mission group that asks for it. It is a gift from the East to the West—an opportunity extended.

Now is the time for the family of God to link hands around the world. It is time for us to lay aside what was, to look at what is, and then to look forward to what will be. It is time for each of us to be willing to not only teach but also to be teachable. It is time for the financially blessed among us to loosen our grip and pour out the finances that will enable those with wide-open opportunities to make the most of them. It is time to support each other so that together we can bring in a great harvest for the Lord.

We are the family of God.

❧

"But seek ye first the kingdom of God, and his righteousness; and all these things shall be added unto you."
—Matthew 6:33, KJV

CHAPTER 11
EAST MEETS
WEST

A force of forty thousand trained Christian witnesses armed with a strategy to reach every one of India's more than four thousand unreached people groups. Indian missionaries moving into Burma, and Bhutan, and Tibet, and Nepal; down to Sri Lanka; and up to the Arab states of the Persian Gulf. African believers receiving training and then using it to reach their brothers and sisters for Christ, even in African countries where the population is largely Muslim. Asians trained and then taking the gospel to other Asians. Right now the good news of Jesus Christ is spreading into unreached corners of the world in innovative and exciting ways.

Not many people will be surprised to hear that the West's passion for missions has cooled in recent years. One exception is short-term mission trips on which many churches are sending groups, especially young people. They go to places such as Haiti and South America to build orphanages. They conduct youth camps in various African countries. They pack their musical instruments and Bibles and head out to participate in evangelistic outreach teams around the globe. They teach English; they help on medical teams; they participate in sports outreach programs.

And in a reversal of what we have come to think of as the traditional approach to missions, a smattering of missionaries are coming from the East to serve in the West—Nigerian missionaries at work in Ireland, for instance, and South Korean missionaries operating in the United States. It is indeed a whole new day for missions.

Western Christians are easily caught up in their enthusiasm for mission conferences, elaborate programs and productions, and short-term trips, without pausing to ask their brothers and sisters around the world what would really be helpful to them. Is all that short-term building really worth the investment of time and money it takes to fly an entire group of teenagers and their sponsors halfway around the world? Would the time of these evangelistic teams be better spent training nationals to conduct outreach events, rather than Westerners doing it themselves? What benefit are those flashy productions, anyway? Could there be other approaches that might better meet the needs of partner countries? What important concerns have well-meaning Westerners failed to consider?

In short, *what do Christians in the two-thirds world need from their brothers and sisters in the West? How can East and West work together in a more effective way?* And since Vijayam has spent so much of his life on the front lines of global missions, he and his team seem to be in a good position to provide answers to these questions.

Yes, Vijayam agrees that times certainly have changed. Gone are the days when Westerners simply moved to another country to work as missionaries. Today, it is increasingly difficult for them to gain direct access to the people who most need to hear the gospel. This is certainly true in India, a country that will not issue visas for mission work.

These changes are not necessarily bad, as we saw in the last chapter. In many countries, the presence of Western missionaries simply perpetuates the myth that Christianity is the religion of the West. Furthermore, many people around the world who are eager to drink American soft drinks and wear American jeans want nothing to do with other things American, especially religion. Even more importantly, once Western missionaries are gone from a country, the national church has no choice but to step up and take the vacant leadership roles, pushing local Christians into positions many feel they should have been holding all along.

So with this new paradigm in mind, what can Christians in the West do to help nurture and strengthen their brothers and sisters in countries such as India? And what information will enable them to be effective, caring partners? Christians in the West can learn to understand history, they can put a priority on responsible action, they can become global partners, and they can pray.

Let's take a closer look at each of these.

Learn to Understand History

Because their own national history is relatively brief, Christians in North America especially need to be reminded that to understand the present, they must begin to look at the past. A particular area's demographics, its attitude toward Christianity, its response to anyone perceived as Christian—each of these is usually rooted in history.

India is a good example. During nearly two hundred years of mission efforts under colonial governors, the majority of the work reached only a few specific cultural groups and members of the high castes. Masses of people in rural areas, ethnic sub-cultures, tribal groups, and minorities were routinely passed over. Little wonder, then, that it is mainly the tribal peoples who make up India's thousands of unreached people groups. Neither should it come as a surprise that they are largely illiterate and generally live in a state of poverty unimaginable in the West.

But let us step back even further, for the medieval crusades cut a swath so deep, it will forever scar the face of Christianity. And to look at events without recognizing the importance of that still-angry scar—or to sigh impatiently and simply say, "Oh, get over it!"—is to court disaster. When U.S. President George W. Bush made the decision to wage war in Iraq, the East saw it as a breach of international law with clear ramifications for Israel. It was an act that immediately raised the specter of the crusades. People with economic and political interests rushed to form alliances, followed by eruptions of terrorism. The East watched as, for the second time in history, the Muslim heart was lost.

The reaction did not come from Muslims only, according to P. T. George. At the same time that Islamic terrorism was rising, Hindu terrorism accelerated against Christianity, and this situation continues to grow in India.

So the first word from the East to the West is one of warning: It is imperative that Christians in the West understand history and that they appreciate its importance. For unless they do, history is bound to repeat itself in tragic ways.

Put a Priority on Responsible Action

Few of us would argue the importance of being committed to responsible actions. We desire responsibility of ourselves, and we expect it of our partners.

Sometimes, however, responsibility can become a cloudy issue. For what one side automatically condemns as irresponsible behavior, the other may accept as merely an unfortunate human frailty, or perhaps a cultural problem, or just a result of history.

Past Actions

If Western Christians are to understand their brothers and sisters in the East, they must grasp the damage left from the violence, exploitation, and atrocities in the two-thirds world perpetrated through the years by Christians. Many in the West will be quick to respond: "Why dredge that up? Past is past. Let it go. Pick up, and go on from here."

What they fail to understand is that such an attitude trivializes a horrendous past. In India as well as in many other countries, the cry is for Christian leaders to step up and apologize for what was done in the past by Christians. Such an action would be seen as the West finally accepting responsibility. And it would go a long way toward opening lines of communication that have been sealed off for far too long.

Present Actions

Doing my best to avoid making a mess, I awkwardly wiped the plate I held in my lap with the remains of my chapati, then I scooped the last bites of rice and curry into my mouth—what I didn't spill down the front of my clothes, that is. I couldn't blame young Stephen, who was sitting next to me, for giggling at my clumsy efforts to eat Indian style.

We shared a wonderful Indian meal with three generations of the Vijayam family. My husband, Dan, and I gathered with the Vijayams in their home, joining their four children and sons- and daughter-in-law. All the grandchildren were there, too, except for Junia, the oldest, who was away at college in California. The other girls—Sheba, Maureen, and Sharon—sang for us; then we all sang "His Banner over Me Is Love." After that, Dr. Vijayam read a chapter from the Bible, and then grandson Joshua led the family prayer time.

In the Vijayam home, every evening is the same. Not that the entire family always gets together, but whoever is there joins in evening devotions. Always. It's a family legacy passed from generation to generation.

"My parents taught all their children to get up early in the morning, sing songs of praise—some of them composed by my father—and read the Word of God in our family prayer meetings," Vijayam recalled. "It is the way we started every day. And we also ended the day with family worship."

The Western church has a great deal to offer the church in the two-thirds world. In many ways the West remains a bastion of global influence and power. It is the source of an array of materials and resources. And its donors provide financial assistance to Christians around the world. Yet, patterns of behavior seen in Western Christians are causing great concern in other parts of the world, not only because they are weakening the church in the West but also because those patterns are spreading to the East. One of the most worrisome of these patterns is the breakdown of the family, the basic unit of society and the church.

When Vijayam was young, his mother put the last of the wood logs on the fire to cook breakfast. She asked her children to do what to her seemed the only natural response when faced with a desperate family concern: pray together. During their regular prayer time that morning, they simply asked God to supply their need. And before they left the kitchen, a new supply of wood arrived.

When Bunyan Joseph faced the abrupt end to his honored career as Bishop of the Church of South India, his children watched as he laid the situation before the Lord and then calmly went about the business of serving God.

Vijayam looks back at the family in which he was raised, at Mary's and his family, and at many other Christian families, and he credits the firm grounding in prayer and Bible study for carrying them through the hard times. And he speaks of the church leadership and the high standards they set for themselves and for the people.

Such a foundation is hard to find in the pressure-driven West, where regular family prayer and Bible study are increasingly rare. "In this modern world, there just isn't time," harried parents insist. "Not with the kids going in so many directions. Not with so many demands on our time. It's a good idea, but we just cannot do it!"

Indian Christians wonder, *Could that be one reason for the weakening family in the West?* They look with disbelief at the soaring rate of divorce and separation in North America. "It is just as high among believers as non-believers!" one Indian man exclaimed incredulously. "Even pastors and church leaders divorce and remarry, and then they continue on as pastors and leaders, as though nothing had happened. How can such a thing be?" And they wonder, *If Christians sit by and do not demand responsible behavior from their leaders, are they not themselves acting irresponsibly?*

Adele, whose husband is a pastor in Egypt, said, "You in America have a responsibility to the rest of us. The way you dress and the way you behave. The movies you watch without protest. Your casual attitude toward family responsibility. Everyone in the world watches you and hears what you say. Then everyone says, 'Oh yes, now we know what Christians are like because we have seen Americans.'"

Religious leaders in the West also bear a responsibility for the soundness of the Christian message being preached from their pulpit and spread around the world. Too many teach that

God promises earthly prosperity to his people. Some go so far as to say, "In heaven I will not need gold; it is on earth that I need it." And while they claim to spread the gospel, they are amassing great riches from gullible followers who prefer that message to the words of Jesus: "Do not store up for yourselves treasures on earth, where moth and rust destroy, and where thieves break in and steal. But store up for yourselves treasures in heaven, where moth and rust do not destroy, and thieves do not break in and steal. For where your treasure is, there your heart will be also" (Matthew 6:19–21).

A few leaders go so far as to suggest that any person who struggles financially is simply demonstrating his or her weak faith. Imagine the impact of such a message coming out of the comfortable West, where opportunities and resources are plentiful, and then spreading eastward into countries where life itself is a daunting daily challenge.

Such leaders go on to teach that Jesus promised that his followers would receive back a hundred-fold on whatever they give away. As evidence, they quote Jesus' words from Mark 10:29–30: "I tell you the truth, . . . no one who has left home or brothers or sisters or mother or father or children or fields for me and the gospel will fail to receive a hundred times as much in this present age (homes, brothers, sisters, mothers, children and fields—and with them persecutions) and in the age to come, eternal life."

Did Jesus mean that faithful sacrifice would be rewarded with literally a hundred times outpouring of money? If so, what about the "brothers and sisters" part of his words? Will the faithful also be rewarded with a hundred times the number of brothers and sisters? How about mothers and children?

A "hundred times" is not the most important phrase here. More important is "with persecution." Certainly, Christians have suffered persecution since the first century. But did those believers actually enjoy prosperity in this world? The Christians who were forced to leave everything and hide in the catacombs might argue that point, as might Sadhu Sundar Singh and Gideon Bunyan and Bunyan Joseph. Even today many around the world face persecution for their faith, including many in India. Are they heaped with earthly rewards?

If people were less eager to find a promise of earthly riches, they would consider the question in light of the entire thrust of Scripture. For instance, in Luke 6:20–23, Jesus told his disciples, "Blessed are you who are poor, for yours is the kingdom of God. Blessed are you who hunger now, for you will be satisfied. Blessed are you who weep now, for you will laugh."

As we have seen, some faithful followers of Christ have been richly blessed with earthly wealth. But they should in no way see their situation as payback for their great faith or good works. Many other equally faithful Christians have not been blessed in a material way (Jesus' disciples included). Certainly, that does not mean God's hand isn't on them also or that their faith has in some way faltered.

We in God's family are repeatedly warned against putting our faith in earthly possessions. "For we brought nothing into the world and we can take nothing out of it. But if we have food and clothing, we will be content with that. People who want to get rich fall into temptation and a trap and into many foolish and harmful desires that plunge men into ruin and destruction. For the love of money is a root of all kinds of evil. Some people, eager for money, have wandered from the faith and pierced themselves with many griefs" (1 Timothy 6:7–10).

Become Global Partners

As Vijayam prepared for a staff prayer meeting, a friend confronted him with a litany of frustrations about U.S. Christians and their response to politics. "If you were in America you would see things differently," Vijayam told him. "Perhaps," his friend said. "But I was born in India. Why did God show me the examples of Sundar Singh and Bunyan Joseph? At a time like this, is it not our part to witness boldly from the place God put us?"

Exactly! Different views from different positions in which God has placed his children. This is one of the major benefits of a partnership. Especially now, when we are living in an Acts 13 world. Especially now, in a time of transition, when the old rules of influence have shifted.

Fortunately, many mission agencies have given up the paternalistic, "we-have-the-answers" approach, and in its place they have adopted the partnership approach. Besides, Westerners can no longer go as missionaries to most of the countries that are home to the majority of the world's unreached people. Most of what is referred to as the 10/40 window—the imaginary band named by Luis Bush to designate the area across Africa and Asia from 10 to 40 degrees latitude north of the equator—is not open to Westerners. But others *can* go.

Consider Moala, who treks all along the foothills of the Himalayas to take the gospel to isolated tribes. And Amit, who braves the evils of black magic in order to tell the tribal people in Orissa about Jesus. And Nilesh, who walks to every single house in his entire area of Maharastra. And Haopu, who labors and witnesses in Bhutan. These people belong to the area in which they minister, or at least to related areas. They understand the cultural taboos. They may know the language or dialect of the people, and they fit in well enough to move around freely. They know what they must do to be accepted in the community. No Western missionary could begin to do what these local people can do.

The shift in mission approach actually started in China, back when that country's doors closed to foreign missions and refugees fled to places such as Hong Kong. Sponsor a Child was one of the earliest programs to shift the emphasis toward partnership. Many Christian National Evangelism Commissions (CNEC) were organized in many countries. Later these were organized worldwide to form Partners International.

A prominent missionary to India coined the phrase "Neither *above* you, nor *below* you, but *with* you." But Partners International took the concept one step further. They saw the high quality of people in their partner countries, and they began to look to them as mentors. Vijayam was one of these.

"The world has changed dramatically since those days," Jon Lewis said of this post-9/11 world. And Partners International's definition of partnership has changed with it. Now Jon Lewis defines it this way: "Partnership is a two-way bridge between the resource-rich and the opportunity-rich."

No longer is the missions effort a flow from the West to the East. No, now it is a resource exchange, and it goes both ways. This is why it is so important that the church in the West gains a better understanding of itself from the viewpoint of the two-thirds world—and gains an appreciation for what the two-thirds world has to offer the West. These same insights are also vital for the church in the East so it can accurately understand Western Christians.

From an effective partnership come increased communication and mutual learning. The folk methods of communication used at MERIBA could be recorded and passed along for others to use, for instance, in Africa, in Cambodia, and also in the United States as it seeks ways to work with its immigrant population. What originates in India can become a valuable learning tool in cultures far different from its own. The JVI materials designed to train Master Trainers are an excellent example. Already they are in use in many areas of the world, such as Senegal, Sri Lanka, Indonesia, Canada, and the United States.

When we come together in the spirit of Acts 15—old ways along with new, Western ways along with those of the two-thirds world—we can debate, and we can listen. We can come to the place where we work it out together. Because we all have the same goal—accomplishing the Lord's work.

Prayer

And finally—but by no means least—we can pray. Actually, to commit ourselves to faithful intercessory prayer is the most effective thing Western Christians and Western Christian organizations can do for their partners in the East. And likewise, it is the most effective thing Christians in the two-thirds world can do for their partners in the West. James 5:16 assures us that "the prayer of a righteous person is powerful and effective" (TNIV).

Ask the Indian indigenous missionaries who are carrying God's Word into hostile lands what their greatest request is and they will almost uniformly give the same response: "Please pray for me." They are heading into extremely dangerous situations, yet their first request is not for safety. Because they come from poor families, the majority of the missionaries constantly struggle to gather enough finances to support themselves, yet their first request is not for money. They want most of all to know that they have people committed to pray for them and for their work. For they know that God alone can provide safety and health and finances as well as wisdom and clarity of thought and everything else they need.

Also, when we pray for our partners, God will answer our prayers by showing us what other steps he would have us take. Prayer is something each of us can do without ever leaving home. It's something the rich can do, and it's something the poor can do equally well. The educated can pray, and so can the illiterate. We can pray in large cities and in rural areas, in the East and in the West.

And a special benefit awaits partners who commit to pray regularly for each other. A deep, caring bond will naturally develop between them. What a wonderful gift for partners to give each other!

⁓

"Now to him who is able to do immeasurably more than all
we ask or imagine, according to his power that is at work
within us, to him be the glory in the church and in Christ Jesus
throughout all generations, for ever and ever! Amen."
—Ephesians 3:20–21

CHAPTER 12
THE TIME IS
NOW

Mahatma Gandhi in India. Nelson Mandela in South Africa. Martin Luther King in the United States of America. William Wilberforce in Great Britain. Wang Weilin, the young man who stood in front of an advancing column of tanks bent on crushing a prodemocracy demonstration in China's Tiananmen Square. Throughout history, great social reforms have come about because one person refused to say, "It is not right, but this is how it has always been. And, really, what can one person do?"

Esther. Joseph. Moses. Peter. Paul. Martin Luther. John Newton. Sundar Singh. Bishop Bunyan Joseph. Billy Graham. Brother Yun in China. Throughout time, imperfect and unlikely people have been used by God to rouse his people to action.

Moses Swamidas in India. Rene in Senegal. Mike in Ireland. Chui Pau in China. Reverend Jordan in Birmingham, Alabama. Sharon Elliott in Los Angeles, California. Right now, this very day, things are happening all around the world because ordinary people, whose names are not known and who have never attracted headlines, are stepping forward to devote themselves to a cause. For example, a Dalit in India refuses to accept that entire segments of people are inherently inferior and should stay in the gutters. An African engineer gives up a prestigious government job to serve God in an area where Christians are not welcome. An African-American, in Christ's name, champions social justice in America's deep south. A dedicated high school teacher devotes her talents to offering inner-city kids a hope and a future. Each one of these is quietly going about the business of living and serving in the place where God placed him or her. Each one says, "Here I am, Lord. Use me."

Around the world, there is a cry for justice and mercy. It is calling for people to boldly and humbly walk with God.

We live in challenging times. But then, all times are challenging for those who are willing to make a mark for God. For each of us, the time we are given and the place in which God places us presents us with options.

- We can mind our own business and bend all our efforts toward caring for our family and making a good life for ourselves.

- We can shake our head, cluck our tongue, and decry the pitiful state of the world's affairs. We can argue over how things got so bad and who is to blame for the problems. Then we can comfort ourselves with the assurance that we, at least, are safely on God's side.

- We can offer a general prayer for everyone around the world who suffers and goes without. Then we can reach into our pocket to contribute a few bills to a relief effort so we can feel good about having done our little bit to help—before going on with our life.

- We can step forward and get to work.

In a world of growing fear, despair, and cynicism; in an age of reason; and in a culture too sophisticated and savvy to believe in the miraculous intervention of God, Christians around the world are called to rediscover the compassion of Jesus. He walked and talked with the poor, he healed the sick, and he championed the oppressed. Just as in the time of Ezekiel the prophet, in this age—when officials of many countries both in the East and the West act like "wolves tearing their prey, shedding blood, killing people for unjust gain"—the Lord is again looking for some-one to build the wall and stand before him in the gap (Ezekiel 22:27–30). Christians are called to grasp anew the truth of what God can do with one person who is willing to jump to his or her feet and proclaim, "Here I am, Lord. Use me."

B. E. Vijayam went from a worried little boy bouncing across the countryside in the back of his papa's bullock cart to an angry Marxist communist determined to force justice by rebellion, to a respected scientist in a secure university position, to a nationally acclaimed humanitarian, to a man who answered God's call to step into the gap.

"But I'm not like Dr. Vijayam," you may be saying. "I am no scientist. I don't have his contacts or his knowledge. And, besides, if I were to decide to lead, no one would follow me."

Ask B. E. Vijayam about his credentials and how God has used them and he will tell you, "I can very clearly see that over the years the Lord was preparing me for the great vision he has now given me to establish his kingdom."

Vijayam's single most important asset is not his natural abilities, or his training, or his contacts. No, it is his willingness to make himself available. It is simply his great desire to be a useful instrument in the Lord's hands.

Every person can offer his or her professional skills, talents, social concern, and spiritual commitment to the Lord. Imagine God using these people . . . the African-American teenage boys being challenged to get an education, to become responsible citizens, and to be the next generation of church leaders, all because of the efforts of Reverend Jordan. Imagine the kids who will be writers, or educators, or ministers, or champions of social justice because Sharon Elliott considers teaching more than just a job. Imagine the Dalits in South India unifying, refusing to stay in their place, and moving forward in the name of Christ because of the leadership of Moses Swamidas. Imagine, in areas where the population is over 95 percent Muslim, churches being started and leaders being trained because of Rene's faithful work in Senegal and beyond. Imagine the excitement of the Irish folk who hear Mike passionately explain the grace of God and what it means for them. Imagine Chui Pau's neighbors in China who come to enjoy a cup of tea and leave knowing Jesus Christ. Imagine you doing whatever it is God gifted you to do, and imagine God seizing your efforts and multiplying them many times over for his kingdom.

"But my efforts simply are not worth that much," you may insist. Great! Perfect! That puts you in total agreement with the apostle Paul who wrote: "But we have this treasure in jars of clay to show that this all-surpassing power is from God and not from us" (2 Corinthians 4:7).

The problem with great talents and abilities is our all-too-human tendency to grasp our successes and hold them high, to flaunt and wave them around, eagerly pointing out our accomplishments to anyone who will listen.

In the apostle Paul's day it was customary to hide one's valuables in a worthless, old clay jar that was so ordinary and drab it would never attract the attention of a thief. In the same way, the tools for spreading the gospel throughout the earth are hidden in the most unsuspected place—in us—ordinary people who do ordinary things, every ordinary day of our ordinary lives. Except that when our talents are given to God, the ordinary is transformed into something extraordinary. It becomes all-surpassing power.

Talk to Vijayam about all that he has accomplished and he will quickly remind you that it was possible only because of the encouragement, prayers, and cooperation of his wife, Mary Chinthamani. He is right, of course. The fact is that no one but Jesus could accomplish the work of the Father alone. Each of the great people we mentioned from history and each of the men and women whose stories are recorded in the Bible had others who worked alongside them. And it's the same for each of the men and women who are making a mark today. We accomplish kingdom tasks together.

Perhaps there are those who are ready to work with you. They may have already felt God's nudge and are only waiting for you to step forward and lead the way. Why not begin today to pray for the people God will bring to work alongside you? It matters not that you don't yet know who they are. And consider this: some future helper may already be praying for you.

Should you have the opportunity to go to India and spend time visiting the rural areas, you might be tempted to say to Vijayam, "After a lifetime of working on behalf of the poor, the oppressed, and those who don't know the name of Christ, there certainly seems to still be an awful lot to do!"

And Vijayam would agree. But then he would remind you that Indian Christians across the country are actively challenging the traditional taboos of their society: the illegal but deeply entrenched caste system, the dowry payments required for a family to get a husband for their daughter, and the philosophy of karma that forever locks the poor and ill into guilty hopelessness. Vijayam would take an entire day to tell you about Indian Christians who are taking the gospel of Jesus Christ to areas that, only a few years ago, no one even considered possible areas of ministry. He would take you on a hill at JVI to look out over Carmel and watch the breeze rustle across grassy fields and ruffle leaves in the grafted trees, all hanging heavy with fruit. He would explain new developments, new technologies to help the poor.

Even as Vijayam speaks, you would hear the chickens clucking behind you, and off to the side, the soft bleating of sheep. Products of top animal husbandry developments, he would point out. Then he would walk you around the campus, and whatever the day, whatever the season, it would be bustling with life. Men in their area and women in theirs, studying, or worshiping, or learning technologies from the scientists, or practicing what they were learning. All busy preparing to expand the kingdom.

And then Dr. Vijayam would likely ask, "And how about you? Do you know the Lord as your personal Savior and Lord? Will you give your time and talents to serve him in his kingdom?"

Because every one of us has a role to play.

ℰℐ

"For if you remain silent at this time, relief and deliverance for the Jews will arise from another place, but you and your father's family will perish. And who knows but that you have come to royal position for such a time as this?"
—Esther 4:14

EPILOGUE

On my last day in India, I joined the Master Trainers and the IWILL women at the Carmel campus chapel for early morning worship. Someone handed me a songbook, but I couldn't read it. The songs of praise were all in Hindi, and even though the words were printed out before me, I wasn't able to follow—except when we came to the words *Hallelujah!* and *Amen!* Those words I knew, so I really sang them out.

Evidently, Vijayam noticed, because he said, "*Hallelujah* and *Amen* are heavenly words. They are the same in every language. One day we will all be singing those words around God's throne in heaven!"

Then the young man leading the worship said we would sing one more song, "God Is So Good." But first, he asked everyone to call out his or her native tongue. As they did, he wrote the following languages on a flip chart:

- Hindi
- Gujarati

- Tamil

- Assamese

- Bengali

- Boru . . .

The list went on and on until twenty-two languages were listed. Twenty-two native tongues in that room, and only one native English speaker—me. Then we sang, all together, but each in his or her own tongue. We sang the song through once. It was so beautiful, our languages weaving and blending into a verbal harmony.

Evidently, I wasn't the only one who was moved, because as one, we raised our voices and sang it again. When we finished the second time, we sat in silence. But only for a minute. We all stood to our feet, loudly poured out our melting pot of voices, and sang it a third time. "That's what heaven will be like," the worship leader said when we finally recovered.

I wondered if the apostle John heard anything like that accompanying his great vision of heaven? If not, he is in for a great treat.

☙

"After this I looked and there before me was a
great multitude that no one could count, from every nation,
tribe, people and language, standing before the throne
and in front of the Lamb. They were wearing white
robes and were holding palm branches in their hands.

And they cried out in a loud voice: 'Salvation belongs to
our God, who sits on the throne and to the Lamb.'"
—Revelation 7:9

❧

Hallelujah!
Amen!